A Bad Case of Capitalism

by

Shiraz Balolia

Published 2020
Printed in Canada
ISBN: 978-1-7923-5470-0
ISBN: 978-1-7923-5471-7

First edition

Contents

Dedicated to the reader who has a dream.

This book is meant to energize young and older minds alike, and dispel thoughts that you cannot be successful without outside help.

Everyone has inner strength and determination
that can be brought out.

I wrote my story to help you discover your own.

Note

This is a true story. There is no fiction in this
autobiography.
Some names have been altered.
Dialogue remains true to the spirit of what happened.

From Inc. magazine, 1996

While You're Reading This, He's Starting Another Business

An entrepreneur who currently runs eleven different companies explains why he has such a bad case of capitalism.

"I see opportunities out there that are so easy, I can't help myself," says Shiraz Balolia. Maybe that's why Balolia runs eleven companies in addition to Woodstock International, a wholesale distributor of woodworking tools. The Kenyan-born entrepreneur's enterprises range from cutlery to jewelry to sculpture to real estate development. To gain an edge on his fellow cutlery retailers, Balolia started Grizzly Knife & Tackle, a wholesaler—which supplies products to retailers. He hopes Grizzly will be able to count "almost every single one of our competitors" as a customer.

"I have a bad case of capitalism," he says.

A Bad Case of Capitalism

CHAPTER 1

Socks, Notes, and Open Windows

My heart pounded as I stared up at my father, his face tense with fury. I shrank behind my two older brothers, making them a shield between me and our father, who stood over six feet tall.

I was seven. My brothers Anil and Akbar, twelve and sixteen, stood in front of me on the concrete stairs leading up the back of the building to our second-floor apartment.

Father took a step toward my brothers, and the heavy metal-grill door to our apartment slammed shut behind him. He grabbed Akbar's wrist in one hand and Anil's in the other, looking at what they held. Father's voice came out in a growl. "Where did you get these?"

My brothers' hands each held a pair of socks. New socks. Socks that had lain moments before on a top shelf of the first-floor mercantile store below our apartment. Socks near an open rear window, next to the concrete stairs we three had just sprinted up, only to encounter our father on his way down.

My hands were empty. Years younger than my brothers, as usual I had just been tagging along, and I had no interest in socks anyway. But my innocence didn't quiet my pounding heart as I peeked around Anil. As I clutched Anil's back, I could feel my brother trembling.

Akbar spoke quietly. "We got the socks from the store."

"Which store, and how did you pay for them?" Father's voice was measured, slow, steady.

"That store," Akbar whispered, pointing to the propped-open window near the stairs. "The window was open, they were right there…"

Father struck. His open palm slapped Akbar's cheek, then Anil's.

"Go to the shop owner!" Father snapped. "Tell him what you've done! Tell him you're sorry. Return those socks and tell him to close the window, so others can't do what you have done!"

Akbar and Anil looked down, as their cheeks started to turn red from the slaps. I stayed hidden behind Anil. Silent, we waited for Father to pass, continuing on his way, before my two brothers went down the stairs and out around to the shop front, to face the shop owner.

My father's life was based on honesty and integrity. Over the years, anyone who had dealings with him found him to be honest to a fault. Hassanali Balolia was born in 1920 in a one-room hut with a packed dirt floor and a pieced-together roof of scrap metal, in a rural shantytown near the small city of Barol, in Gujarat state, in west central India. His father Nanji, my grandfather, operated a tiny roadside store—actually more of a shack--close by, selling items such as tobacco, cigarette papers for rolling your own, tea (known as chai), hairpins, matches, soap, clothing, snacks, and the like.

Hassanali, soon called Hassan, was the first-born. His mother Jena, my grandmother, gave birth to three more children but died soon after her fourth child was born, when Hassan was thirteen. My grandfather Nanji never remarried. During Hassan's early years, under British colonial rule in the early 20th century, poverty in India intensified. Most days, food was scarce, and the children often went to bed hungry.

Despite this, Nanji determined that at least one of his offspring would go to school. Scraping together the thirty rupees per month tuition, which included room and board at a hostel, Nanji sent his eldest, Hassan, to school in a neighboring village.

Hassan loved the challenge of academics, excelling in math, but soon enough Nanji could no longer afford it, and abruptly moved him home again. A few days later, one of the teachers visited their one-room home to investigate. Learning the reason, and knowing the boy's potential, he arranged for Hassan to continue at school, free.

Back at school, Hassan faced challenges that weren't academic. He was the only Muslim student living in the hostel. The other boys lodging there were Hindu. They viewed their Muslim classmate through a lens of segregation.

Their ringleader was a powerfully built boy, Jadhav, who feared being seen as weak academically, so he covered up that insecurity with physical bullying and intimidation. The other boys, needing to stay on Jadhav's good side to avoid being bullied themselves, followed his lead. And here was Hassan. A Muslim on his own in the school, with no kin to help. A target.

The beatings started and did not stop. Hassan knew he couldn't physically defend himself against so many. Nor could he let it continue.

Always the thinker, Hassan approached Jadhav, offering to tutor him in math in return for protection. It worked! Soon the other boys joined in Hassan's evening tutoring sessions. When Hassan eventually graduated with high honors, the other boys, including Jadhav, were his friends.

Back at home, living in the hut and working at his family's roadside store-shack, Hassan could see that those high honors would never make any difference if he stayed put. Poverty in India under British colonial rule had grown even worse during the 1920s and '30s. He'd heard opportunities were better in British East Africa, across the Arabian Sea and Indian Ocean, an area that included Kenya, Uganda, and Zanzibar plus Tanganyika, now known as Tanzania.

For young Indian men like Hassan, British East Africa looked like the New World. At age twenty, barely out of school, but already wearing the neat suit and tie of the bookkeeper he would become, in 1940 he emigrated from India to Mwanza, Tanzania. Others from India's Gujarat state, many of them merchants and traders, were already moving there.

Like immigrants everywhere, Hassan chose to settle in a neighborhood alongside other newcomers from his homeland. Like bookkeepers everywhere, he had no trouble landing a job almost immediately. He gained employment at the Ismaili Community Council, a local governing body responsible for education, health, housing, and youth development for this moderate sect of Islam.

Gregarious and outgoing, Hassan soon became a familiar face in his Gujarati immigrant neighborhood in Mwanza. He'd no sooner arrive home from work than he'd hear a knock on his door, and open it to find one or two of the community elders, come to ask if he'd do some accounting for them in the evenings. As a young single man with evenings available, and eager to make extra money, he always said yes.

But those available evenings, and his single status, wouldn't last long.

Every weekday including Saturdays, Hassan walked the half-mile to the Ismaili Community Council office in Mwanza. His route took him down dusty, noisy streets, with old houses set right next to the dirt road he traversed. He didn't notice, at first, that a curtain at the window on the same house, day after day, would flick open just as he passed.

Hassan was six feet one inch tall, young and handsome, and in that suit and tie, obviously well employed. None of that was missed by the girl behind the curtain. She watched, day after day, until she worked up the courage to flick back the curtain, catch his eye, turn her chin up to one side, and smile.

It was a bold move for Nurbanu, the 14-year-old girl behind the curtain. Girls did not talk to boys, and they certainly didn't talk to young men like Hassan, who was twenty-one. But it worked. A few days later, Hassan passed her a note written in Gujarati, which Nurbanu could read. Soon notes were being exchanged frequently. As was common for the time, they did not address each other directly. But Hassan knew a good thing when he saw it, even if it was mostly hidden by a curtain. He went to the community elders, asking them to speak to Nurbanu's parents on his behalf.

Nurbanu was one of eighteen children, only seven of whom (six girls and one boy) survived into their teens and beyond. Her widowed mother had now determined that her daughters would marry well. As the sole adult breadwinner for her large family, Nurbanu's mother was definitely interested in the potential of the good-looking, professionally dressed Hassan. Such a marriage would ease her financial burden by taking Nurbanu off her hands, but would he love and cherish her daughter? And Nurbanu was still so young. It took several visits from the elders, and finally Hassan in person—he and Nurbanu still did not speak directly—before the widow agreed to her 14-year-old daughter's immediate marriage.

Despite the age difference, my parents' marriage was a happy one, resulting in four children. The first three, son Akbar, daughter Yasmin, and son Anil, came quickly, each two years apart. Like the parents, the three children quickly integrated into their neighborhood, and grew accustomed to the community elders who still dropped by in the evenings, asking Hassan to do their bookkeeping. One of those elders, a businessman who owned enterprises throughout East Africa, recognized the young man's talent and offered to pay for Hassan's college education back in India, to make him a full-fledged accountant. The offer included living expenses for Hassan and his family while there. In return, Hassan would have to do the books for all his businesses for no charge, as long as the businessman was alive.

Hassan leapt at the chance. Though it would mean moving with his wife and three children back to India for the duration, it was still a wonderful offer. Hassan and his family moved to Bombay, India, where Hassan earned his auditing and certified accountant's degrees before returning with his family to Mwanza three years later.

But now, to Hassan's eyes, little Mwanza, Tanzania, looked more than ever like the very small town it was. Meanwhile, he was hearing talk--via those extensive and connected Indian immigrant communities throughout East Africa—of good opportunities for accountants in neighboring Kenya, in the coastal town of Mombasa. Might he and his family move there, and continue doing the books of the businessman who'd paid for his education? He could!

Once again, with his wife and three children, Hassan moved toward opportunity. In Mombasa, he launched his own accounting firm, where his reputation for fairness quickly spread. He was known as "the honest accountant," and when anyone in town mentioned that term, others knew they meant Hassan Balolia. He hired other accountants, and business flourished.

As his company grew, so did his family: in 1952, when my siblings were five, seven, and nine, Hassan and Nurbanu welcomed me, their youngest and final child.

Father, Age 21 (1941)

Left to Right

Front: Anil, Aunt, Yasmin, Grandfather, Shiraz (on horse), Akbar, Mother

Back: Uncle, and Father

A Bad Case of Capitalism

CHAPTER 2

Tropical Mombasa and Education

My siblings and I tumbled into the dining room, chattering and laughing, our dinnertime appetites whetted by the aroma of Mother's cooking. On this normal, warm weekday evening in the tropical city of Mombasa, Kenya, as usual Father in his suit and tie took his seat at the far end of our big, Formica-topped table. Mother, in her printed housedress, her lovely round face smiling at us, sat at the other end nearer the kitchen. At five feet one inch tall, Mother was a bit hefty now; she was as short and gentle as Father was tall and forceful. On the table in front of her now, the fragrant, familiar Indian dish of sabzi, full of vegetables and spices as only Mother could make it, made my mouth water.

I looked at the other dishes: savory chicken curry; matar pilau, which is rice and peas with caramelized onions and aromatic cloves and cinnamon; and best of all, a glass dish holding Mother's homemade mango pickles. My siblings, all teenagers, quieted as Father thanked God for the food. I, eight years old, kept still too, though my stomach rumbled loudly.

As our plates were filled, then emptied, then filled again with second servings, the lively soundtrack of my siblings chattering in our particular dialect of Gujarati filled the room. I joined in. "Pilau dio," I asked, which was "Pass the rice." My sister Yasmin reached to pass me the dish, but Father's arm shot out and his hand clamped her forearm.

"No!" he growled, and Yasmin left the dish where it was. The room fell into pin-drop silence.

"At the dinner table, Shiraz is to speak only in English!" Father said. "Only if he asks in English will the food be passed to him!"

Unfair, I thought, though I said nothing. Why were the older kids allowed to speak in Gujarati? Why was I the only one forced to speak in English? My lower lip jutted out, and I slumped against the stiff-backed wood dining chair.

"Shiraz, sit up straight, and ask in English," Father snapped.

I sat up. "Please pass the rice," I said, meekly. Yasmin passed the dish, and the soundtrack of chatter started up again.

Father took charge of another aspect of our education: swimming lessons. These started a couple of years earlier when I was six, near the Old Port of Mombasa. The Old Port had seen many centuries of sailing ships, and still accommodated trading vessels such as the graceful Arab dhows.

Every morning at 6 a.m., five days a week, Father would drive with my brothers and me toward the Old Port. Nearby, watching over the harbor, stood Fort Jesus, built in the 1590s by the Portuguese. Fort Jesus has a long and macabre history, and today is a UNESCO World Heritage site, but on those early mornings in 1958, that designation was still far off in the future. This morning, we saw only the usual fleet of dhows anchored close to the wooden docks of the Old Port, plus a large rowboat waiting for us to row it out to a floating pontoon in the middle of the harbor.

About fifteen other community members were also arriving. We all piled into the rowboat and shoved off, a couple of the adult males rowing, heading toward the pontoon.

I'd been coming along on these swim outings now for about a month. This early in the morning, it was chilly enough so that I hugged my arms about me as I sat packed in among others on a splintery bench in the boat. Once we arrived near the big pontoon, one of the men let down the anchor sixty feet to the ocean floor, and others around me jumped and dove into the sea. I leapt in too, wearing my arm floaters as usual, paddling around for a few minutes before grabbing the gunwale of the boat and hoisting myself up over it and back in.

"Shiraz, today you will swim without floaters," Father spoke to me, in

English as always, as he tugged off my arm floaters.

"No, no, no!" I yelled, suddenly panicked, but my floaters were quickly gone. Father picked me up and threw me into the water. I went under but came up, gasping and yelling, thrashing my way back to the boat. I grabbed the gunwale of the boat and quickly pulled myself back in.

My father picked me up and threw me in again.

"No!" I yelled once more. But this time, in that micro-second while I was airborne, I saw that I would splash down in the midst of a circle of eight men, all of whom were treading water, watching me. In that split second, I realized Father must have asked them to do this, in case I didn't swim.

But this time, I did. Maybe it was because I realized I hadn't drowned the first time. Maybe it was because I was ready, which Father knew but I didn't. But whatever the reason, I stopped thrashing and started paddling. The men around me treading water started to clap, as did my brothers up on the pontoon. My father, watching me from the boat, just smiled and said, "There you go, you know how to swim."

After that, I left my arm floaters behind and swam freely with the others, in that old harbor with its graceful Arab dhows, under the watchful eye of the ancient Fort Jesus.

Growing up in an Indian community in Mombasa, attending a school structured around the British education system, we four children spoke three languages: Gujarati, Swahili, and English. Father, who spoke Punjabi and Hindi as well, was determined that the four of us would excel in the English language. Under his influence, the language skills of my older siblings developed really well, but by the time I came along, Father had further honed his ideas about how to develop a child's excellence in language. He decided I could only speak with him in English, and moreover, was not allowed to speak any other language at the dinner table.

Of course it was unfair—that was all I could see at the time--

but it was also brilliant. Thanks to my father, I excelled in English at school, bringing home grades with high distinction. My English skills were further developed because I loved to read, and often read novels when I arrived at school early, or during lunchtime. I liked both British and American authors, including Earle Stanley Gardner (I read just about every Perry Mason book), Harold Robbins, best known for "The Carpetbaggers," and James Hadley Chase, who wrote thrillers. The American books acquainted me with some of the slang. I also got hooked on another author, Tuesday Lopsang Rampa, with his unusual book "The Third Eye." During my final test in Form IV in Mombasa, I wrote a story for the essay part of the exam about a man at a bar getting into trouble. Since it was the finals, our exam papers were sent to England to be corrected by British teachers. I received a distinction (equivalent to an A+) in English and a note from the person who corrected the papers "this boy has a lot of imagination."

But it was Father's methods that had the most effect. His English-only rule at the dinner table was not the only result of being the sole young child in a family of teenagers. Growing up as the baby of the family, my gentle mother, who cooked some delicious treats for the family, continually urged me to "eat, eat," which I loved to do! Not surprisingly, I became a chubby child, whereupon my ever-strict father admonished me to "exercise, lose weight!" He did not allow me to eat any candy, or sweets as they were called.-

But one thing both parents agreed on wholeheartedly was the value of education. Education had enabled my father to rise from crushing poverty into the comfort and security brought about by his professional endeavors. Where education was concerned, neither parent was about to let any one of their children become slackers. All four of us attended the same rigorous private school. The headmaster was a former British Army Colonel, Mr. Cockry. That was his real name.

The academics at that school were stellar, but Headmaster Cockry was a tyrant. His favorite tool for punishment was a three-foot-long bamboo cane, half an inch in diameter. Any pupil who was insubordinate, in any way, would have to report to Cockry's office, where the unfortunate but deserving "victim" would hold out both hands, palms up. A few times, I was on the receiving end of that cane. One time, all I'd done was throw small pebbles (OK, they might have been sizeable rocks) at my friend…while he was seated on a school bus, next to a window. Why did that bus window have to be so fragile, and why did that teacher have to just come around the corner and see the whole thing? Oh well. My resulting trip to Cockry's office left my palms so swollen and purple with bruises that for a few days I couldn't hold a pen to write. But I soon realized that in holding my palms out steady for the cane, I was one of the lucky ones.

The sound of bamboo swishing through the air, whistling with speed toward a kid's outstretched palms, inspired legendary fear among us students, so much so that some pupils would involuntarily pull their hands back. But that only made it worse. I once witnessed a classmate stand before Cockry for this punishment. As the headmaster raised his arm up and back so the bamboo cane would descend with full force, my classmate yanked his hand back and dodged sideways, leaving the cane to whistle harmlessly through the air. But that was a huge mistake. As the boy sprinted around Cockry's office, Cockry kept after him, beating the boy on his back and all over his body, over and over again. It was hard to watch!

Nowadays, even in Kenya, a headmaster like that would be jailed.

We had school every day until 4 p.m., and Saturdays until 2 p.m. The school uniform for boys, in the tropical steaminess of Mombasa, was khaki shorts, a white, short-sleeve shirt, white socks, and black, properly polished shoes; girls wore a grey skirt, white blouse, and white socks. Their hair had to be neatly tied in a ponytail. School wasn't all studies and sticks. We loved soccer, which we called football, and played it every day at lunchtime and after school. We also played field hockey. I was not the fastest runner, but I had quick reflexes, and was chosen for hockey goalkeeper.

Partly due to the school's academic rigor, and partly due to my father's influence, I became a regimented person who values order, fairness, and efficiency. But that's tempered by my mother's influence, who instilled in me her quiet sense of generosity. In every city and town we lived in, unbeknownst to my father, she always found time to volunteer for the community welfare society. As the youngest, I spent a good deal of time with her, absorbing intangible values as well as learning practical skills of cooking and sewing. I learned to sew on her old treadle-powered machine. This sewing machine, lacquered black with Singer in gold lettering, was powered by a foot pedal. That pedal drove a flywheel on the machine, which helped even out the power and speed. The sewing skills I learned from my mother reinforced an aptitude for working with my hands.

Our home in Mombasa was in a neighborhood that included people of different faiths and nationalities. Christians, Hindus, and Muslims lived in harmony as good neighbors; when anyone brought food to another as a gift, they'd keep faith in mind, bringing no meat to a Hindu family, no pork to a Muslim one. My best friends across the street belonged to a Catholic family of five boys and two girls. Sometimes, a couple of them would show up to our evening soccer games in the street, rubbing their backsides and muttering about "Scrooge." It was the name they called their father, an ex-French Navy captain, when he pulled out his belt to condition their backsides! They never called him Scrooge to his face. None of us would have talked back to our fathers in any way. I was scared of my own father, which made communication with him difficult.

CHAPTER 3

To Congo with Love

O ne summer evening in the mid-1960s when I was fourteen, with my school holidays just begun, Father called me into the living room. He and Mother had a visitor with them, a short, stocky, middle-aged man with muscular arms and stubby hands. I remembered this man. He was an occasional client of my father's. I'd seen him at our Ismaili mosque, and once at a community picnic, where he entertained us boys with tall tales. At the time, he seemed fun.

He smiled at me now. I smiled back.

My father spoke. "You remember Mr. Shamash?"

"Yes, of course. Hello uncle," I said, using the honorific as a sign of respect, as he was not a relative.

"You're going on holiday with Mr. Shamash," my father said.

What? What!? I had no idea what Father had in mind, but I dared not question him. I looked at Mother, sitting silently. Her face was closed, and she looked distressed.

"Mr. Shamash owns a hotel in Beni, Congo," Father went on. "You'll be helping out around the hotel for a month. Pack your bag as you will be leaving on Saturday."

Later, when Mother and I were alone, she told me that she was very unhappy with the idea to send me to a different country. I suddenly understood why there'd been a flurry recently to prepare a passport for me. Two days later, we left by car, Mr. Shamash driving. All traces of the friendly funster from the picnic had vanished. Without my parents there, he didn't even try to smile. Or speak. He kept his eyes on the road and his stubby hands on the wheel.

So, I was silent too.

One mile down. More than a thousand miles to go.

We traveled northwest through Kenya and west across Uganda. When we crossed into Congo, his car bumped and jarred over the deep-rutted dirt road as my head bounced violently.

Still I stayed silent, stiffening my neck to prepare for more jolts, until I saw a pole ahead of us, along the side of the road. Six feet tall and slightly askew, it sported what looked like a white soccer ball jammed atop it. As we jounced past, I saw that the soccer ball was a human skull, bleached white by the scorching sun. Stunned, I swiveled my head to look as we drove past. Its eye sockets were vacant, its discolored teeth chipped.

"What's that!" I cried.

"It's what happens to those who resist," Mr. Shamash said, keeping his hands on the wheel, dodging ruts. He swerved to miss a pothole, and I was tossed sideways. Another hundred yards, another pole, another human skull propped on top like a prize.

"The heads are from the revolution," he said, finally turning to me, his face expressionless. After Congo gained independence from Belgium in 1960, the country was rocked by conflicts that were later seen as a series of civil wars. History would name the years from 1960 to 1965 the Congo Crisis, but right now, Mr. Shamash was calling it the revolution.

We drove on, passing skulls on poles every hundred yards.

I shrank into my seat, looking at Mr. Shamash out of the corner of my eye, thinking *where is he taking me?* I had never wanted to go home more than I did at that moment.

"The victors hang up the heads of the losers so others will see them, and think twice about fighting back," Mr. Shamash said.

A few miles further, we saw a crowd gathered. As we drew closer, we saw they were gathered around a massive dead hippo, lying on its side in its blood, next to a soldier lifting his rifle overhead with both hands. The soldier, his face joyful in victory, had one leg up on the hippo's body.

"That's common," Mr. Shamash said. "The soldier killed it so the villagers will have meat. The forces in charge want to show people they'll provide for them."

Mr. Shamash's hotel in Beni was nothing exotic. The main building, built of limestone blocks with brick trim, consisted of a large dining room with a bar on one end, a rudimentary kitchen that smelled of stale grease, small living quarters for Mr. Shamash, and a couple of outbuildings off to one side. The guest rooms were little limestone block cottages behind the main building.

At dinner that night, over ugali (cornmeal cake) and beef stew, I finally learned why I was here. Mr. Shamash said it was my father's directive that I needed to lose weight, and Mr. Shamash was going to help in that regard.

And so he did. I had nothing sweet, no fruit, no fruit juice, certainly no sodas, no potatoes, no rice, nothing fried. If it was pleasurable to eat, I did not get it. The first two weeks were a misery of homesickness bound up by constant hunger.

My stomach grew smaller, my face leaner, and my pants looser, as I worked around the hotel. My duties included receiving, counting, and organizing all the produce that came into the hotel, as well as tending bar. The half-dozen or so soldiers who came in during the evenings thought it amusing that a 14-year-old was bartending. They always counted their change after I gave it to them. It was always correct.

Early in the evening, they joked around with me, but after a few drinks, the jokes would get ruder, the talk rougher, and their treatment of me meaner. One evening, an argument among them escalated, and when I giggled at something, a soldier across the counter tossed a bottle at me. I ducked and the bottle flew past, exploding against the back wall. After that, Mr. Shamash pulled me off bartending duty.

At night I slept, or tried to, on a narrow, steel-famed bed with a thin, hard mattress, pushed up against one wall in a little space off the main room. As I tossed and turned on the rock-hard mattress, my stomach growling, through the open door I listened to Mr. Shamash and a bunch of friends, mostly Greek, play poker, shout, laugh, and drink.

Greeks had long been present in many industries in Congo. After Congo's independence in 1960, most Greek settlers departed; the men still hanging around Mr. Shamash's card table on those nights in 1966 were there for diamonds. They operated transportation businesses, which, along with legitimate trade, were used to transport illegal diamonds.

Night after night, the talk around the card table would turn to women and money. Mr. Shamash would eventually send one of the men out to a particular guest cottage, where a young woman was waiting, and the real reason for the men's visits would become clear. Mr. Shamash, among his other businesses, was a pimp. I didn't know the word yet, though I figured out what was going on.

As time passed, one day rolling into another, I longed for home, but when that endless month finally ended, Mr. Shamash said he wasn't available to drive me back to Mombasa.

On the afternoon I was to depart, an ancient, army-green truck rattled up in front of Mr. Shamash's hotel and slammed to a stop.

Two men quickly exited the driver's side and passenger side, leaving their doors open. I grabbed my bag and stepped aside of the dust cloud following the truck. I watched the two strangers, one about twenty, the other middle-aged, trot one after the other into an outbuilding by the hotel. Each returned holding an ivory tusk, which they quickly stowed under the truck's front bench seat. They asked me to get in.

I gripped my bag. "What is that?" My question felt almost involuntary. All I knew was there were two ivory tusks under the spot where I was supposed to sit.

The older man, his eyes bloodshot, his rough skin pitted, his beard stubbled, turned to me. "Nothing you need to worry about," he snapped. "Nothing you saw. Now toss your bag back there and go sit in the middle."

I did as I was told. Mr. Shamash was not there to wave me goodbye.

We reached the Congo side of the Congo/Uganda border about 8 p.m. The beard-stubbled driver, without direction from anyone, immediately pulled to the side where border guards stood at ease, their rifle butts in the dirt, in front of a few huts, with a few women and children hanging around. As the beard-stubbled driver opened his truck door, his demeanor instantly changed. With the guards, he was not gruff, but jovial. He and the other man seemed to know them well. From deep in the truck, behind the seat, they retrieved bottles of booze, a crate of shoes and slippers, and a case of dried fish. Toting these bribes, my two seatmates disappeared with all the guards into one of the larger huts.

I sat alert in the middle of the seat, not wanting to move for fear that the tusks may be discovered. I kept quiet and ignored the women and children going about their business around the truck.

About forty-five minutes later, one of the border guards exited the hut. Clutching a bottle in one hand and his rifle in the other, he veered toward me. A couple other guards, laughing, stumbled out of the hut after him. Some of the women paused to watch. It was later now, and the little children had vanished.

"Hey. You!" he yelled at me through the open driver's side window, waving the bottle, sloshing the liquid. "Come out! Come with me!"

"Why?" I asked. "Where? Where are we going?"

"Get out of the lorry and I will show you!" he barked, swigging from the bottle. I slid off the bench seat and jumped down onto the dirt road. He pointed to a girl, about my age, leaning against the hut. She was smiling at me.

"That's your bibi (wife)," the guard said.

I felt a wave of panic. "She's not my bibi!" I leapt back up onto the seat, my face flaming. As I quickly closed the truck door behind me, I heard a roar of laughter from the guards.

Eventually my driver and the other passenger/smuggler said their goodbyes. We drove a few hundred yards in the dark to the Uganda side of the border, where—after similar bribes to similar guards—we were mercifully waved through into Uganda. Mr. Shamash had pre-arranged the different legs of my journey and my lodging, and the beard-stubbled driver now dropped me off at the small house of an Indian family in the town of Kasese, Uganda where I spent the night. Next day, I was picked up by four more strangers, three men and one woman, who drove me to the city of Kampala, Uganda. It was evening by the time we arrived, and they dropped me off in front of the local mosque.

I was still 400 miles from home. I had nowhere to stay and nowhere to sleep. The mosque was deserted except for a caretaker sitting in his tiny office. He said I could sleep under the open veranda of the mosque, and there was a straw mat available I could use.

I spread the thin mat on the cold stone floor outside the mosque and laid down. No blanket. Equatorial Kampala, at nearly 4,000 feet elevation, is generally pleasant unless you're sleeping rough outdoors, when the night-time temperature can drop below 60.

To this day, I remember what an uncomfortable and frigid night that was.

Next morning, the mosque staff offered me breakfast of two fried eggs, bread, and tea with milk and sugar. Afterward I walked the few blocks to the train station. Mr. Shamash had given me thirty shillings for the trip, of which the train ticket to Nairobi would be twenty-five. After I bought the ticket, I had nothing to do until the train departure at 6 p.m.

I saw a sidewalk magazine seller who had comic books laid on the sidewalk, and I bought one for one shilling. Within an hour, I'd gone through every square inch of that comic book.

What to do? I had four shillings left. I was not about to blow that on more comic books. I looked again at the comics, fanned out on the sidewalk before me. It was barely 9 a.m. The day looked as if it would be full of loneliness and boredom.

I addressed the merchant in Swahili, suggesting a deal. Could I exchange the comic book I had just bought for another? I would read one, return it for another, and at the end of the day, I would leave the last one with him. I promised I would return each book in like-new condition. He agreed.

When I was ready to board the train, I handed him the last book, shook his hand, and thanked him for trusting me. It was the perfect deal: he made one shilling profit without selling any merchandise, and I got to read seven comic books for one shilling.

The train was an overnight sleeper. I had no money for dinner that night, nor breakfast next day. I settled for a bag of plums at the train station, spending one shilling on it, before arriving in Nairobi next day at 8 a.m. Using a public phone in a phone booth, I called one of my cousins, who lived in that city. I spent a few days with my cousins and aunt before borrowing train fare from my aunt, and finally boarding the train to Mombasa and home.

My mother was overjoyed to see me. She rushed from the house, an energetic missile of happiness in her floral housedress, through our front garden onto the driveway, and enveloped me in hugs. Neither she nor my father had been aware I was traveling home without Mr. Shamash until I was in Nairobi, when my aunt had called my mother. Mother was understandably upset, but relieved now.

My father was happy to see me too, if much more reserved. He was certainly pleased that I'd lost fifteen pounds under Mr. Shamash's feeding, or lack thereof.

But the lost weight didn't stay off more than a year, in large part due to my mother. She went right back to her usual behavior, urging me to "Eat, eat, poor baby!" Father was dismayed, but—thankfully—he did not send me back to Mr. Shamash.

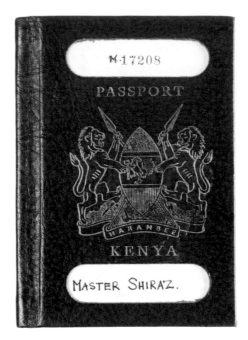

Shiraz's Kenya Passport - Age 14

	Mwenye Pasi *Bearer*	Mke *Wife*
MAELEZO *DESCRIPTION*		
Kazi *Profession* }	STUDENT.	
Mahali pa kuzaliwa *Place of birth* }	MOMBASA. KENYA.	
Tarehe ya kuzaliwa *Date of birth* }	25. 6. 1952, *See observation page*	
Mahali aishipo *Residence* }	KENYA.	
Urefu *Height* }	5 ft. 4 in.	ft. in.
Rangi ya macho *Colour of eyes* }	BLACK	
Rangi ya nywele *Colour of hair* }	BLACK	
Alama yo yote isiyo ya kawaida *Special peculiarities* }	SCAR ON THE LEPT KNEE!	

WATOTO *CHILDREN*

Jina *Name*	Tarehe ya kuzaliwa *Date of birth*	Mume au mke *Sex*

Sahihi ya mwenye Pasi *Signature of holder* } *Baloti*

Sahihi ya mke *Signature of wife* }

Picha ya Mwenye Pasi *Photograph of Bearer*

Picha ya Mke *Photograph of Wife*

(PICHA) (*PHOTO*)

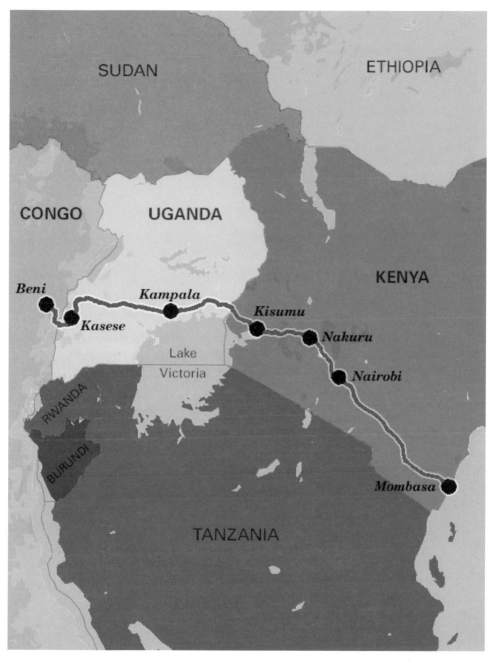

Map of Journey to Congo

A Bad Case of Capitalism

CHAPTER 4

Mombasa to Nairobi

In Mombasa, as in our previous town of Mwanza, my father's reputation for fairness and common sense was well known. Not only did he own the accounting business, he taught accounting classes on Saturdays, and had also bought a laundry and dry-cleaning facility that employed seventy-five workers. Pearl Laundry & Dry Cleaners was large enough so that it operated more like a factory. It was well-situated near the harbor in Mombasa. Mombasa itself was an island connected to the mainland by a causeway. Ships came into Mombasa's harbor and needed laundry services, delivering hundreds of sheets, pillowcases, blankets, tablecloths to Pearl Laundry. We would turn them around within a day, as ships stayed in port only a short time.

Thus, like children of merchants and business owners everywhere, I gained an education not only at school, but by helping at the family business after school and on weekends.

The sheets and other laundry were washed in gigantic machines, but it was the ironing and pressing rollers that loom large in memory. One big roller was nicknamed "Nyama Choma" by the Swahili-speaking workers. The name means barbecued meat. At Pearl Laundry, Nyama Choma was a massive cylinder four feet in diameter, wider than a full-size bedsheet, solid steel, and extremely hot. Two workers would feed a wet, fresh-laundered sheet in one end, and it would emerge dry and pressed on the other end, where others would fold it, and log it in for return to the correct ship.

When I was at the feeding front of that roller, and working fast, occasionally I would accidentally brush my knuckles or fingertips against the searing hot cylinder. Decades later, I can still feel Nyama Choma's scalding burn. Barbecued meat, indeed!

Because we had a gardener and another domestic worker at home, plus I worked alongside native Swahili speakers at Pearl Laundry, I was getting better in the local dialect of that language. When my school started offering classes in what I thought was Swahili, I was pleased, and thought I'd do well. I began learning all these new and interesting words, such as *semper, ignarus, salve magistra,* etc. I was looking forward to springing them on our gardener when I got home. It was enjoyable until the third class, when I realized it was a Latin class! The other kids went nuts with laughter when I told them I thought I was learning new Swahili words.

As it turned out, I flunked Latin, along with most of the rest of my class. It may have been because Headmaster Cockry was teaching it. Plus, I couldn't see the logic of teaching Latin in Africa!

At school, I did well in my favorite subjects of English, math, and physics. I liked geography; it was fun to see the different countries, and color them in the workbook. With most history, I didn't see the point of memorizing all those dates; the only part I enjoyed was learning about Dr. Livingstone coming to Africa, establishing trade and religious missions, and eventually becoming an anti-slavery crusader.

The first few years at school, we wrote with fountain pens only: no ballpoint pens allowed. Four days a week, after school let out at 4 p.m., I went for an hour of extra tuition in penmanship (two days) and physics (two days) with private teachers who lived near our home. After that, I was free to play soccer, which we called football, until 6:30 when I stopped play to clean up for our 7:30 dinner. After dinner, I did homework until 9:30 bedtime.

We had a single, small, black-and-white TV set. Programming was terrible. Only two channels were available, and the only thing worth watching, to my mind, was "Mission Impossible." Father let me stay up until 10 p.m. once a week to watch it.

Saturdays, I was in school until 2 p.m. After that, I had free time, which I often filled with guitar practice or pick-up games of football.

Sundays meant a day at the beach with family. We would all pile in one car and leave for the beach around 8 a.m. Mombasa's Bamburi Beach was our favorite hangout with its wide sandy beach, fringed by palm trees. It offered a welcome respite from the tropical heat. My favorite pastime was looking for seashells first thing in the morning. When the tide went out, the beach would stretch several hundred yards deep, leaving behind little puddles of seawater with tiny fish trapped in them.

Mother always packed a nice lunch of samosas, some type of rice-and-vegetable dish, chevdo (a tasty fried snack of potatoes, chickpeas, lentils, nuts) and other Indian snacks. Fresh coconuts were readily available for thirty cents from local beach vendors.

In the late afternoon, we went home to shower, then out again in the evening with the family to the drive-in cinema for an Indian movie. Once again, Mother packed lots of food in the picnic basket for the movie. Life was good!

Between the accounting business and Pearl Laundry, Father's reputation grew. Community members knew where we lived, and as the years passed, people still came to our home in the evenings to seek free advice from him on any subject: money troubles, family disputes, business dilemmas. Once again, the immigrant communities' word-of-mouth grapevine throughout British East Africa spread the news.

When Father heard about an accountant in Nairobi, Kenya, who wanted to retire and sell his business, he determined it was an auspicious time to sell his healthy Mombasa accounting business and buy the bigger one in Nairobi. In late 1968, he moved with his family to that capital city, the largest in Kenya, 300 miles northwest of Mombasa.

Except for me. Once more, my position at the bottom of the family dictated my situation. In the British school system, I was then in secondary school, also called high school, which consisted of years called Form I, II,

III, and IV. I was in Form IV, which is the equivalent of about 12th grade in the American system, but I was sixteen. (I had skipped a grade in primary school. Plus, the British system, with its longer days, meant we were further ahead academically.)

I stayed behind in Mombasa to finish Form IV. In an echo of my father's own schooling, decades before in Gujarat, India, that year I lived in a hostel near the Mombasa school, before moving at year's end to join the family in Nairobi.

In Nairobi in 1969 at age seventeen, I started what would be my last two years of school, Forms V and VI, also known as A levels in the British system. Form V1 was about equal to a first year in college.

Nearly grown now, I had my father's height and my mother's heft, but I was agile at sports. My mother had taught me badminton, and in Nairobi I became the school's badminton captain. At school every lunchtime, we played volleyball in the school courtyard, still in our uniforms of khaki pants, ironed white button-down collared shirt with a maroon tie, and a green blazer of light woven wool with the school emblem on the left chest pocket. (The girls had the same uniform except with a grey skirt.) The uniforms were smart-looking. We would be called out by the teacher if we were out of uniform, or if our uniforms were dirty or not properly pressed, and usually sent home to change into proper clothing

I always removed my jacket and tie before playing, and kept an extra pair of khaki uniform pants in my desk drawer at school, as one of two things would happen during our aggressive lunchtime volleyball: the pant knees would get dirty from all the diving, or the seam around the seat would split. If the latter, I'd tie my green blazer around my waist to walk back into the classroom, fetch the second pair, and go to the boys' room to change. That evening at home, I'd sew up the split seam.

The girls, watching our volleyball games, would get quite the chuckle from our various mishaps.

I enjoyed the challenge of school and sports, but I was angered when classmates thought that because I was overweight, I must also be stupid. One afternoon after class, my friend Zul, with two girls (Shamim and Dilsy, the smartest girls in class and good-looking, too) asked me to take an IQ test.

"What's an IQ test?" I asked.

They couldn't help giggling. Shamim raised her eyebrows and smiled, giving Zul an "I told you so" look. Dilsy tossed her shoulder-length hair and said, "Follow us to the library."

They told me an IQ test measures intelligence. I told them there was no such thing (I was from a small island--what did I know?) but they convinced me that a series of questions existed that could measure a person's smarts. They laid the test before me, then sat there while I wrote answers, which took forty-five minutes.

They checked the results. They looked at each other.

"Well?" I asked. "What do the results tell you?"

"There must be some mistake," Shamim said, frowning. "You'll have to retake it."

I didn't have time that day, but by this time I wanted to know whatever it was they knew. Shamim and Dilsy convinced me to take a similar test the following week.

The week passed. I took the test. In the library, Shamim and Dilsy bent over, their hair swinging forward, to check the results while Zul looked on, silently.

They looked up. Neither spoke.

"Well, what does it say?" I asked.

"These things sometimes don't work properly. There's something wrong with this test, too," Shamim said.

"Forget it!" I said. Fed up, I stood and gathered my bookbag. "I told you, you can't measure intelligence accurately."

Later, Zul told me both tests were real and the results accurate. The two smartest girls in class were surprised and disappointed that my IQ score was higher than theirs.

After that, Shamim and Dilsy at least had the good grace to say hello to me in class.

After school I was usually busy with more productive endeavors. My father's new accounting business in Nairobi was flourishing, but he'd also noticed a need for a modern dry-cleaning store, and having experience in that industry, he opened one. The Apollo series of space missions by the USA was getting a lot of press, and my father named his new venture Apollo Dry Cleaners. Once again, I pitched in at the family dry-cleaning business. I'd head home from school, grab something to eat, and head out to Apollo, where I worked until 7 p.m. During busy seasons, I'd be there until midnight or later, processing loads of dry cleaning and getting them ready for pressing the next morning. I never thought anything of it, that those hours might be unusual for a high school student. I simply understood it was work that needed to be done.

Though I had a key to the house to let myself in, on late nights as I returned from Apollo, my grandmother Janbai (whom we called "Nanima" for maternal grandmother) would shuffle to the door to greet me, then immediately turn and move toward her room, her endearing, side-to-side, rocking walk reminding me of a penguin, as she repeatedly mumbled in Gujarati "Kevo mahenatu chokaro," which translates to "What a hardworking boy!" Eighty years old then, she was waiting up to make sure I got home safely. (Nanima, who bore eighteen children before she was widowed, lived to nearly 100.)

One night I got home about 1 a.m. to find every dog in the neighborhood, about fifteen of them, lounging around our German shepherd, Papoose, in our front yard (or front garden, as we called it). Our home was a single-story rancher, a long and narrow single-story house, in the Parklands neighborhood, three miles northwest of downtown Nairobi. Parklands, then as now, had a significant population of Asians (South Asians, meaning from India), many of whom kept a dog for security. Our Papoose was the friendliest dog ever, beloved by all other canines. I imagine there was no security at any neighbors' homes that night!

Nairobi was rougher than Mombasa. During the three years I lived there, 1969, 1970, and 1971, as crime rose, it seemed increasingly dangerous for Asians. Panga gangs (toughs wielding machetes) attacked, robbed, and slashed their victims. My friends and I knew better than to be out alone at night; we traveled in groups of three or four, borrowing my mother's car to drive to the snooker hall or a disco joint in downtown Nairobi. One friend, a DJ at the disco, had a regular American customer who supplied him with the latest records from the USA. They were at least three months old but sounded new and fresh to us.

Whether we were heading out for snooker or music, I carried a switchblade in my pocket and kept a cricket bat in the back seat. But I wouldn't need to do that forever. With Kenya growing less stable, as I finished A levels and graduated in 1971, my family was thinking more seriously about departing the country.

Apollo Dry Cleaners - 1970, Nairobi

1969. Shiraz, Age 17, in School Uniform in Nairobi:
Khaki pants, green blazer, white shirt, maroon tie.

CHAPTER 5

Done with School

We didn't move away from Nairobi immediately. Right after graduating, I got a job in Nairobi with a hardware importing company. My task was to calculate the cost of all imported shipments: chain, locks, hinges, screws, bolts, and the like.

The business was owned by four brothers, all of whom were present at my job interview. They asked question after question and seemed satisfied with my answers. Then the eldest brother asked what my father's name was.

"Hassanali Balolia," I answered.

Eldest Brother looked at his siblings and spoke without bothering to lower his voice. "This one won't last long," Eldest Brother said. "His father is an accountant and owns a business here. This boy will leave us to join his father's business."

I got the job anyway.

There were no electronic calculators then, so I worked a mechanical calculator that looked like a full-size, ancient typewriter. It was a noisy contraption. Every time a division was made, it blasted rat-a-tat-tat like a machine gun, which irritated the owners. Their offices were right behind my desk, and they could hear the clanging apparatus through the window of their office that faced the back of my desk. But they had supplied the machine for my use, and use it I did, though I checked its division manually afterward.

I applied myself and worked hard. When shipments came in, I stayed late to finish the work, and the owners would eventually ask me to leave.

After a few episodes like this, I asked the manager why the owners wanted me out of there at 5 p.m. even though they were still in the back room.

"They don't want to pay you overtime," he answered.

I went to Eldest Brother and told him I didn't want overtime pay, I just wanted to finish the task at hand. He replied they couldn't let me stay late, as other employees would imagine I was earning overtime. At the time, I couldn't understand this.

I was generally quick at my work. On days when new shipments didn't arrive, I had time to spare, and wandered upstairs to the mezzanine where the accountants and bookkeepers worked, one of whom was a former classmate. The owners saw this, so to keep me busy, Eldest Brother asked the accounting manager to let me audit several years of old ledgers, all handwritten in fountain pen.

I threw myself into auditing them, finding no discrepancies. My classmate, smiling, soon told me the ledgers had already been audited twice by outside firms and found to be error-free. The accounting manager, and entire accounting department, found my newly assigned task humorous, he said.

Riled, I felt the gauntlet had been thrown down. I had learned auditing from my father, the best of the best, and I would not be mocked. I bet my classmate lunch that I would find a mistake in the remainder of the old ledgers.

On the third day, nearly cross-eyed from poring over the handwritten entries, I found it: a 200-shilling error across the row, and yet the total at the bottom that was supposed to be carried forward appeared to be correct. In accounting this is called "pushing the numbers" and making them agree. In my opinion, then and now, any accountant that pushes numbers is dishonest and should be terminated.

I knocked on the office door of Eldest Brother. I showed him the ledger. He looked at the ledger, looked at me, looked again at the ledger. The mistake was right there, in blue fountain pen on creamy paper.

Eldest Brother's face tightened. He sent me out and called the accounting manager into his office. Even through the closed door, I could hear Eldest Brother screaming at the accounting manager. How could he and his whole department miss an error that a kid just out of school could find?

After that, the accounting manager's demeanor toward me changed to a glare every time I passed.

My wages at the hardware store were 800 shillings a month, of which I had to give my mother 300 shillings for room and board. This was Father's decree. I didn't mind. I still had 500 with which I could do as I pleased. On payday, I'd walk across the street to a shop that sold coins, and purchase some for my collection.

I worked at the hardware store three months before Father asked me to work for him at his dry-cleaning store. He would pay the same, but the hours would be longer. "No" was not an option, and I promptly went to work running the dry-cleaning store full-time.

Eldest Brother was right. I didn't last long.

Apollo Dry Cleaners was a modern dry cleaner and somewhat high priced, so our clientele was mostly ex-patriates from Great Britain and Europe. I enjoyed joking and talking with our customers, who often had interesting stories to tell about their work and travel. With employees, all local Africans, I spoke Swahili as I worked alongside them. The only other English speaker in the store was my older sister Yasmin, who was there part-time a few hours per week.

Apollo was in a new area of Nairobi, on the outskirts of our Parklands neighborhood, on the first floor of a mixed-use building with apartments on the second floor, with an empty field across the street in front of it. The store had a glass front, and once inside, customers could see past the counter to the clothes being processed, and the machines to the left of that. The store had the smell of steam from the presses, and the acrid whiff of the chemicals used for spot removal. As customers dropped off their clothes and chatted with me at the front counter, they could see and hear all the activity: the cleaning, pressing, bagging, and the polite "ding-dong" on the door announcing another customer.

I arrived daily at the store at 7:45 a.m., fired up the compressor and boiler, let employees in, and starting processing garments. We were open 8 a.m. to 6 p.m. six days a week. In those pre-computer days, it worked like this: clothes were brought in, tagged with an order number, and tossed into a "dirty clothes" laundry cart; the cart was wheeled to the spotter to pre-treat stains, using different chemicals for blood, curry, ink, and such; and sorted by color before being loaded into our new and magnificent Donini dry-cleaning machine, which had been delivered from its Italian manufacturer a couple of months before. (When we opened the crate, we found two bottles of Donini champagne packed alongside the Donini-made machine, with a note congratulating us on the purchase. I promptly handed the two bottles to my father, who gave them away to a couple of his large accounting clients.)

The Donini cleaned clothes in solvent and sent them through an internal dry cycle, so they came out hot to the touch and needed to be removed immediately. I quickly hung the clothes on a rollaway hanging cart and rolled them over to the pressing crew, who'd steam-press one piece at a time, hang them on another cart, and roll them over to another worker, who used the still-attached tags to sort them according to order number. It was among my duties to check that each order was correct and complete. Overhead were three large rolls of perforated plastic bags; after checking the order, I'd choose an appropriate size, bag the items, and hang them in numerical sequence on our small overhead conveyor.

I attended to customers and collected money, and at day's end, entered every transaction into a ledger my father had set up. Because of this, at any time we would know which orders had been picked up, how much money was collected, and which orders were in process. My father would come on Saturdays to process payroll for the employees and audit my work.

Father was preparing to send me to university in England to become a chartered accountant (the British version of an American certified public accountant). He had me all set for this, when I did something surprising. I told him, no more education.

I had grown up. I had gained confidence. I had my own agenda.

Her name was Leili.

Father Auditing my Work on Saturdays at Apollo

Old Mechanical Calculator, although the one I used was in better condition than this one.

CHAPTER 6

Leili

I had first met Leili two years before, when my family was still living in Mombasa. It was late August, during school holidays, just past my 16th birthday. My mother told me that a daughter of our relative was coming to visit. The daughter, Leili, would be bringing her friend, Nasrin. Both girls were about my age.

The morning they arrived, I was just returning home on my bicycle from a guitar lesson.

I wheeled my bike through the driveway entrance into our home's courtyard. Some months before, with my father's businesses flourishing, we'd moved to this two-story house with its window-mounted air conditioners, off-white stucco walls with brown trim, and ceramic-tile roof. The house and yard were surrounded by a four-foot-tall, barbed-wire fence, and a gate that opened manually to the driveway. A dirt road full of potholes went by the front of our house and gate.

Through the gate into our yard, I pushed my bike around Mother's vegetable beds, and leaned it up against the largest mango tree. Our yard had several varieties of fruit trees; the two biggest bore mangoes that attracted monkeys, who amused us by leaping from branch to branch. Of course, we liked mangoes too, and since I was accurate with my slingshot, I often used it to bring down mangoes for us. But right now, I wasn't thinking about monkeys or mangoes.

I bounded into the house, and saw a beautiful girl coming down our stairs, with another girl behind her. I looked at the first girl and did a double take. She was stunning, with almond eyes, fair skin, and dark waves of glossy hair falling in curls below her shoulders. She was gorgeous. Her face was lit by a lovely smile.

Until she saw me. Her smile disappeared, and she turned ever so slightly away from me.

My mother, saying, "This is my son, Shiraz," didn't notice.

I did. I was used to this sort of immediate snub from girls at school. I always felt it was because I was overweight. I'd learned to ignore it at school, and I did that now.

My reply was neutral. "Hello," I said coolly, nodding at Leili and Nasrin behind her. I went to the kitchen to grab a glass of water, and left to see my friends across the street.

Later my mother let me know I was to take both girls out the next day and show them Mombasa, so next morning, I took seven shillings from my total savings of thirty-five, and the three of us took a bus to the center of town.

We walked around town, past mosques and colorful Hindu temples, around long market tables set up in the shade of trees lining the streets, and past restaurants and shops with their fronts open to the humid weather. Without meaning to, I found we were in front of a tiny cafe that I knew had absolutely the best milkshakes in Mombasa.

"Oh! These milkshakes are so good!" I said. "Really smooth and fresh."

We could see in, where a paper-hatted attendant held a stainless-steel tumbler under a whirring machine. We watched as he poured the frothy creaminess into a tall, ribbed glass, stuck a straw in it straight up, and slid it across the worn Formica counter toward a child sitting on a stool topped with cracked red vinyl.

"I want one!" Leili said, watching the child dip a long-handled spoon into the pink strawberry milkshake.

"Sure," I said, and then to the attendant, nodding first at Leili and then Nasrin, "Two, please, to go."

As we walked away from the café along the sidewalk, Leili took a sip and said it was the best milkshake she'd ever had.

She looked at me. "You're not having one?" Leili asked, eyebrows raised. "I thought you said these were your favorite."

"I'm not really hungry."

Leili sipped on the straw. "This is terrific," she said. "Come on, Shiraz, I can't believe you don't want one." Her eyes narrowed and she tipped her head, looking at me.

"It's like this," I said. "My weekly allowance is one shilling. After bus fare this morning, and two milkshakes, I have four shillings in my pocket. I still want to buy snacks for us this morning, and I need bus fare home for the three of us."

"Why didn't you say something?" Leili stopped drinking the shake. "I wouldn't have had one." She looked at me, her brown eyes locking with mine.

"I'll only drink this if you share it with me," she said, handing me the tall container. I took a couple of pulls on the straw—it was as heavenly as I remembered—and handed it back.

After the milkshakes, we walked through the market, and I offered to buy snacks. Now it was Leili who said she wasn't hungry. I knew she was saying that to spare me more expense. As she spoke, I noticed a subtle shift in the relationship between us. The vibe was entirely different from yesterday's moment on the stairs. It filled me with happiness; joy seemed to bubble up inside me, as I looked at Leili chatting with Nasrin.

I said I would share the snacks with them if she'd let me buy them, so I bought snacks for all, leaving me with just enough money for three bus fares home. On the bus, I sat behind the two girls, gazing at the back of Leili's head, smiling whenever she turned to talk with me.

The next few days were some of the best of my life. I spent them all, full-time, with Leili. We went cycling and swimming together, with Nasrin too, but since Nasrin wasn't the active type, she sometimes chose to sit out. I was thrilled when I discovered Leili was a superb badminton player. I was even more thrilled when I began to realize Leili didn't care that I was a fat kid. She'd glimpsed my heart, that day as we walked away from the milkshake café in Mombasa. She cared about my heart.

Her 16th birthday fell during that nine-day visit. Earlier, I had subtly asked whether she liked perfume. For her birthday, I used the balance of my savings, twenty-eight shillings, to buy her the nicest bottle of the best perfume I could find. She loved the gift, but even more, she was touched that a boy cared enough to find out what she wanted.

I didn't care that the perfume cost everything I had. Her kisses were worth it.

When the time came for the girls to leave, I made a stack of corned beef sandwiches and packed it for their 300-mile-plus bus journey from Mombasa to Dar es Salaam, Tanzania, Leili's hometown. This was one time that my love of eating worked in my favor! After she arrived home, her first letter to me mentioned how hungry they became during their day-long journey, and how tasty my sandwiches were.

To this day, she remembers those sandwiches.

For the next year or so, we communicated via letter, plus the occasional phone call. As I finished my Form IV year in the hostel near my school in Mombasa and moved to Nairobi to join my family, I kept writing letters to Leili.

It was those letters that got me in trouble.

CHAPTER 7

Trouble with Fathers

L eili was an extremely beautiful girl, and this did not go unnoticed in her hometown of Dar es Salaam. As she grew up and approached marrying age, numerous proposals came to Leili's father regularly from the parents of boys and young men interested in marrying her.

Even men several years older than Leili approached her father directly with proposals of marriage for his daughter. Her father, Ramzan, a kind man with a big heart, was naturally protective of Leili as well as her sisters. He wanted Leili to complete her studies, and he envisioned her eventually marrying a doctor or lawyer or similar professional who would make her happy.

The mail system in Africa was based on P.O. Boxes, not physical addresses. Leili's father stopped at the post office daily to pick up mail that included all of his business mail as well as household mail. After Leili returned from her visit to our home in Mombasa, Ramzan noticed an increase in the frequency of my letters to Leili. When my letters started arriving every two or three days, he asked Leili about them.

At first, she said I had become a good friend, but when pressed, she admitted she was in love with me. This was deeply disappointing news for Ramzan, who had envisioned much loftier matrimonial goals for his favorite daughter. He told her she could not marry me.

When I heard about this from Leili, my own disappointment quickly boiled over into rebellion. I fired off a letter, addressed directly to her father, saying that Leili wanted to marry me as much as I wanted to marry her, and I would! Whether he liked it or not.

I dropped my explosive letter in the red metal mailbox outside the nearest post office in Nairobi and felt vindicated—for an hour or so. Then my good sense kicked in. What had I done? My letter suddenly seemed foolish beyond belief. I prayed it would get lost in the mail.

It didn't. Like an arrow aimed at a target, it found its mark.

"What do you see in him?" her father asked Leili, as he paced the worn Persian carpet in the family's living room in Dar es Salaam, waving my impertinent letter. Ramzan Uncle had met me years before when I was very young, since we were relatives, but our interactions were fleeting, and he didn't really know much about me. Until now.

"This boy is fat. He's not well educated," her father said, looking down again at the letter in his hand, my fiery, foolish letter that was solid evidence against me. "He's mannerless!"

Leili, a respectful daughter who loved her father, understood her elder's point of view. She knew he wanted the best for her. But she also knew my letter was not an accurate picture of me. Soon after I'd mailed it, I'd phoned her, warning her the letter was coming, telling her how sorry I was for sending it.

Now she faced her father, staying calm. "He's sorry," Leili said respectfully. "He didn't mean it."

Leili's mother came in from the kitchen, drying her hands on a towel, and addressed her husband. "Ramju," she said gently. "I know this Balolia family well. Shiraz is a good kid, a little stupid for writing that letter, but he seems like a really nice boy."

Their discussion continued, but a father's protective nature is not easily breached. Leili's letters to me paused, and she did not call for weeks.

But time heals, and love overcomes obstacles. Leili decided to take the secretarial course she'd been thinking about—a secretarial course taught in Nairobi. She moved to our city, lodging in a women's hostel.

My mother was very much in favor of my love for Leili. As it happened, she knew the matron of the women's hostel, who was familiar with Mother's work with charities around town. Because the matron trusted Mother, Leili was able to visit our home on weekends, where we could spend more time together.

But now I was having my own version of Troubles With Father. I knew if I fulfilled my own father's wishes that I travel to England to study accounting, I might lose Leili. I was not going to take that chance.

Leili and I talked it over. We both wanted to get married immediately.

I had never gone against my father's wishes, but I did now.

"I don't want to study anymore," I told my father. "I want to marry Leili."

As if in an echo of Leili's and her father's discussion months before, my father was not in favor. He told me I was too young, and not thinking clearly about my future.

So, I played my ace. "Think of the money you'll save," I said, "not sending me to England for years of studying."

He was not impressed with that! His parenting had been all about educating and improving his children, and he was not pleased about being crossed now. But Mother was on my side. Mother helped my father see that my letter to Leili's father was the result of immaturity, nothing more; I was a good boy who'd learned a valuable lesson.

Also, Mother thought Ramzan Bhai (bhai is an honorific term for brother) might view me in a better light if my father phoned Leili's father to talk things over. After much negotiating, my father phoned Leili's father, to apologize on my behalf. Eventually, they were able to discuss my plans for a formal proposal, and suggest that our family visit theirs, to give me a chance to apologize in person.

Finally, things started looking up. In March 1972, my family took the major step of making plans to visit Leili's home in Dar Es Salaam, more than 500 miles south, where I could formalize the proposal—and apologize to Leili's father in person, in front of everyone, which I did.

As the family climate within our home was settling down, the larger political climate in Kenya was growing more volatile. We felt it was becoming particularly dangerous for Asians (South Asians, from India) like us.

Statistics illuminate the story:

In 1962, the Asian population in Kenya was 179,000.

In 1963, Kenya achieved independence from Britain, resulting in eventual economic and commercial restraints on Asians living in Kenya.

In 1969, the Asian population in Kenya was 139,000.

By 1979, Kenya's Asian population had shrunk to just 79,000.

Thirty years earlier, Kenya had beckoned as the land of opportunity for Asians. Now, in the 1960s and '70s, our ethnic group was looking elsewhere, toward Britain and North America.

Our family would become part of that migration.

CHAPTER 8

Coming to America

In the late 1960s, as economic and political restrictions for Asians in Kenya increased, my family began to think about departing the country. In 1969 my father and uncle (my mother's brother) journeyed to North America on a fact-finding mission, to begin scouting a suitable location for us to settle. They tried New York City first, where the first words out of my father's mouth caused a commotion.

Father and Uncle had just picked up their bags from the baggage carousel at John F. Kennedy International Airport. Exhausted from travel, they were walking out of the airport arrivals door, each carrying a bag, when a stranger sprang to their aid. The man was about forty, as tall as my 6'1" father, but much heavier. The man's open winter coat showed a T-shirt stretched over a muscular, barrel-chested torso. Thick, wavy black hair was tucked under a sweatband, and though it was winter, the man gleamed with sweat, as if he'd been working out.

"I'll help you with that," he said, elbowing Father and Uncle aside, picking up Father's bag from the pavement, taking my uncle's suitcase out of his hand.

Such an offer could trigger only one response from my father, and he uttered it now.

"Is it free?" Father asked.

Mr. Sweatband raised the bags high overhead, paused a moment while he looked straight at Father and Uncle, then slammed both bags onto the pavement. Uncle's bag took an odd bounce but held; Father's bag burst open, spraying clothing and other items out through the split seams. Mr.

Sweatband walked away as if nothing had happened.

Father and Uncle bent over, scrambling to gather the spilled items, quickly sweeping everything back into the broken bag. Eventually my uncle broke the silence. "I guess it wasn't free," he said.

"I guess we won't be living in New York," my father responded.

They turned their backs on the city, went back into JFK, bought some tape for the split bag, and updated their departure for the next city on their list: Toronto.

They landed in Toronto in a snowstorm. Used to the tropical weather of Nairobi, the cold hit like a fist. The frigid wind whipped snow against their faces as they exited the airport, carrying their own bags this time. They flung their suitcases into the trunk of the nearest taxi and jumped into the back seat, slamming the door against the storm.

"Is it often like this in the winter?" my uncle gasped.

"Welcome to Toronto!" the cabdriver said, turning to smile at them. "Winter here means snow from November into March certainly, sometimes October to April. You get used to it."

Father and Uncle were pretty sure they wouldn't, but since they'd already arranged to stay with families in the local Indian immigrant community, they carried on with their few days' reconnaissance anyway. Their hosts, sympathetic, eventually suggested they consider Vancouver.

The climate in Vancouver, on the west coast of British Columbia, Canada, remains temperate and often rainy through winter and spring, and pleasantly sunny through summer. Father and Uncle found the city beautiful, with its English influence and prolific gardens. The city itself had fewer than 400,000 residents then, and $30,000 would buy a reasonably nice home. So, Vancouver it was!

Our exit from Kenya took place in stages. In 1970, Father sent my second-oldest brother Anil, twenty-five, to settle in Vancouver first. (My oldest brother Akbar, with his soon-to-be-wife Pat, was living in London. Sister Yasmin, married and settled in Nairobi, did not emigrate.) Anil had an electrical engineering degree, and Canada's immigration allowed easy entry for those with engineering and professional degrees. Anil would live and work there long enough to achieve "landed immigrant" status, about two years, and then sponsor other family members.

In June 1972 at age nineteen, I flew to Vancouver, a few weeks before Mother and Father planned to follow. I stayed with Anil in his apartment on Cardero Street in the city's West End, near beaches and the lively Robson Street.

Besides his day job at an electrical design firm, Anil had a newspaper route, which he transferred to me immediately upon my arrival.

I awakened at 2:30 a.m. every morning and borrowed Anil's car to pick up the bundled papers from dispatch in downtown Vancouver. I memorized the route of which buildings, and which apartments. Starting at the most-distant building, I'd take the papers up the elevator to the top floor and then start running, tossing a newspaper at the door front of every subscriber on my list. I'd sprint down the stairwell to the next floor and keep going, the weight of the papers lightening as I went. It was quite the workout!

I'd deliver 150 newspapers, finishing about 5:30 or 6 a.m. before going back to the apartment to sleep until 8:30. I earned one dollar per address per month.

Vancouver appealed to me. People were nice, groceries were cheap, the water from the tap was the cleanest I'd ever had. The department stores were luxurious, and since I had extra time in those few weeks before Mother and Father arrived, occasionally I'd wander through a store, marveling at the variety and quality of goods for sale. The sporting goods departments in particular drew me. I'd gaze at the deluxe, full-size rifles for sale, remembering the little air rifle I'd had in Kenya, and the fun my friends and I had had shooting at tin cans on fence posts.

Every few days, a letter from Leili—now my fiancée—would arrive. How I treasured them! I'd put the latest letter in my pocket and walk to Spanish Banks, the sandy beaches along English Bay. I'd lean up against an ancient log, and only then would I open her letter, going through it slowly, making it last, reading it over and over.

I wrote her as often, and she kept my letters.

Mother and Father arrived in Vancouver and bought a single-story house with a finished basement on 47th Street. Leili came to Vancouver in October, and a month later, in November 1972 when we were both twenty, we were married.

The wedding was much less elaborate than it would have been in Africa. We had a little civil ceremony in the courthouse before the registrar, followed by a reception attended by seventy-five people, mostly acquaintances of my father and brother.

I didn't care who else was there. I had Leili, and that was what mattered.

Father quickly settled in Vancouver and soon bought a dry-cleaning business. I got the fulltime job of running it, and Leili and I moved into the basement of my parents' house. Anil, who married after I did, lived with his new wife in the first-floor, three-bedroom section of the house.

My salary from the dry-cleaning store was $400 per month, of which $150 went to Mother (again, at Father's directive). I had just bought an old used Chevy for $400, so I now had a car payment in addition to other expenses, and I was in the red every month.

And Leili was pregnant! We were thrilled, as was Mother. Father was less so. He was sitting at his desk, managing bills, when we told him.

"What were you thinking?" he shouted, throwing down his pen. "You should've waited until you could afford a family!"

I kept quiet. I figured he'd come around once Mother talked to him. Though I was the youngest of my siblings, this would be their first grandchild.

We were all happy to be in Vancouver, but life with two parents and two newlywed couples packed in one house was not easy. There was always some drama, and Leili seemed to catch the worst of it.

A bright spot was the warm relationship between Mother and Leili.

Mother was an excellent cook; she'd even taught cooking classes, back in Mombasa, and won accolades for innovative dishes she created. Leili enjoyed learning from her, and eventually expanded her culinary skills even beyond Mother's, making delicious kuku paka (coconut chicken with a couple of hard-boiled eggs dropped in the sauce), gost ni akhni (a delicious beef and rice dish), and one of my favorites back then, fish cutlets, which she still makes every year for my birthday.

As soon as our son Shabir was born, we wanted to live on our own, but with a newborn, money was even tighter. I applied for low-income housing--and was accepted! We moved into a tiny apartment, paying $150 monthly rent.

I was still making only $400 per month at the dry-cleaning store, so I started cleaning carpets in people's homes. I'd close the store at 6 p.m., go home and quickly eat, then go out to clean carpets until 10 p.m.

It was not lucrative. I made $8 to $12 for cleaning a couple of rooms in a house. After paying for machine rental and cleaning solution, I cleared $50 to $60 per month. It wasn't enough! We squeezed everything we could out of the budget, and still we fell short. Month after month, we had to do without things we needed.

I allotted Leili $10 per month for clothing and incidentals, but instead of spending it on herself, she bought clothing or toys for Shabir.

How could I make more money? That question was always with me. I started taking on alterations at the dry-cleaning store. Now, any evening that I wasn't cleaning carpets, I was at home mending garments. How useful it was that I'd learned to sew from Mother so long ago!

It seemed I was working constantly. In the winter-time, I never saw daylight, since I went to work in the dark and came home in the dark, except for Sundays. That day I kept for family time—and for reviving an old hobby, which I'd started back in Kenya when I'd had that air rifle: target practice.

Wedding Photo - "Fat Kid gets the Stunning Beauty"

November 1972, Leili and I, both 20 years old.

This book went to press on our 48th Wedding Anniversary!

CHAPTER 9

Target Practice

I squinted through the sights of my new Italian-made Bernadelli pistol, holding it with both hands, resting it on the sandbag in front of me at an outdoor shooting range in the suburb of Burnaby, outside Vancouver. It was a chilly, damp, autumn day, and I was in an open-sided wooden shed with a wood-shingled roof over six stalls. In one of the stalls, I sat on the hard stool, looking out across the grassy meadow of the shooting range, viewing the wood target frames at ten, twenty-five, fifty, and 100 yards. Hanging on each frame was an 18-inch-square sheet of paper with a black bullseye, three inches in diameter. I'd chosen a target of twenty-five yards, same as the guy in the stall next to me.

I shifted on the stool, braced myself, and focused on the bullseye. I exhaled slowly and squeezed the trigger.

"Bang!"

Nothing! The paper target on the frame remained untouched, just rippling slightly with the air movement. I sighed, flexed my shoulders, and took a deep breath. *Steady,* I told myself. *Relax.*

I looked at the guy in the next stall to the right of me, also aiming twenty-five yards. He was a few years older than I. He was short, maybe 5 feet 6 inches, solidly built, with dark blond, short-cropped hair and a strong, angular face. He was standing, his left hand tucked into his pants pocket. In his right hand, held out in front of him, he held a Smith & Wesson .44 Magnum pistol (the same model used by Clint Eastwood in the movie "Dirty Harry.") He pulled the trigger and nailed the center of his target.

Wow, I thought. *If he can do that standing, with one hand holding that huge gun, why can't I hit the target seated, with two hands, with my tiny gun resting on a sandbag?*

I rested my pistol on the sandbag again, squinted, exhaled, and squeezed the trigger.

Missed again! Damn!

I glanced again at the guy on my right. He repeated his sequence, his bullet once again piercing the center of his target.

Time for a cease-fire. At this shooting range, every twenty minutes, all shooters were required to move away from their guns as the targets were changed. The guy on my right laid down his pistol, took off his plastic earmuffs, and came over to introduce himself. His name was Wolf Heidemann.

That chance meeting with Wolf at the shooting range in Burnaby changed my life in a way I never imagined.

Wolf, in a thick German accent, asked me if I'd ever shot that pistol before. I hadn't. I hadn't had any sort of gun since leaving my little air rifle behind in Africa a couple of years before. My Bernadelli was new. At $32, it had taken many months of saving to purchase it. Plus, before I could buy it, I had to get a permit from the Vancouver police department.

Wolf showed me how to aim the pistol. "Look at the front sight of the pistol, then look at the rear sights on that Bernadelli," Wolf said. "You want the post of the front sight centered between the posts of the rear sight. Make sure the top of the front sight and rear sight is aligned in a perfectly straight horizontal line."

I did as he said, holding my pistol up toward my target.

"Okay," Wolf said. "Aim the horizontal line of the sights at the bullseye."

I sat on the bench and positioned my pistol on the sandbag in front of me. I relaxed my shoulders, my arms, my mind. I breathed in, then exhaled slowly and pulled the trigger.

"Bang!" My shot was on the paper! Not in the center, but on the paper, and that was progress.

"OK!" I was delighted. "Let's try that again."

"Bang!" I was on the paper again!

"Bang!" a third time, and my shot ripped through the paper, this time near the bullseye.

"Thank you!" I was thrilled with my progress.

Wolf went back around to his stall. We carried on shooting, until the next cease-fire when he came over again. He asked where I was from. He told me about his work; he was a machinist at a German-owned machine shop in Vancouver. I told him I was recently married, with an infant son. Time flew by.

I looked ruefully at my empty box of bullets. Two dollars' worth of ammo, gone in an afternoon.

"It's really expensive, isn't it?" I said. "It doesn't take long to use up a box."

"I make my own ammo," he said. "It's way cheaper, and I shoot a lot, so it's worth it."

"How would you do that?" I had no idea anyone could make bullets at home. If he could, maybe I could too.

"I do gunsmithing at home as a hobby, and I have equipment in my basement I use for reloading ammo," Wolf said. He explained that a round of ammo and a bullet is not the same thing. The bullet is the copper tip that flies out of the barrel when a gun is fired. What remains behind is the brass case. That can be refilled, or as Wolf said, reloaded, into a full round of ammo. This round of ammo is half the cost of a new one, since you don't have to buy the new case of brass, which is the most expensive component. As he explained, I pressed for more detail.

"Look," he said, "why don't you come over this evening and I'll show you the equipment and how it works? Bring your wife and baby. My wife Elaine would enjoy meeting her. We have a 3-year-old daughter, Grace, so we're used to kids."

That evening, Leili and I with Shabir went to their house, and right away our wives started talking babies. Wolf told me that the equipment was in his basement. As we descended the stairs and entered the basement, I saw a machine sitting on top of a bench.

"What's that?" I asked.

Wolf replied it was a lathe.

"What's a lathe?" I continued, with further curiosity.

"A lathe holds and turns round metal objects," Wolf said. "I use it for gunsmithing: threading gun barrels and shafts, and making bushings, which work like bearings to reduce friction between metal parts."

Besides his day job at the machine shop, Wolf worked another business from home in the evenings, as I did. Only his was a lot more profitable than cleaning carpets, shortening pant legs, and replacing zippers. Wolf took old pistols, mostly German-made Lugers, chambered new barrels for them, reapplied the bluing, and did whatever it took to make them work, and look, like new. Then he sold them for a nice profit.

My first glance at the lathe, though, was all it took. I had to have a lathe. But I had no money and could not even begin to afford one.

Wolf at age 21

A Bad Case of Capitalism

CHAPTER 10

Window Shopping

Just because I had no money did not mean I could not look at lathes. In the mid-1970s, Greater Vancouver had a weekly local magazine called Buy & Sell where people listed anything they wanted to sell: sofas, washing machines, tools, used cars, you-name-it. Every Wednesday at 1:30, as soon as the tabloid was delivered to the convenience store across the street from Busy Bee Dry Cleaners, I'd walk over and buy a copy for twenty-five cents. Back at Busy Bee, quite busy myself with loading the dry-cleaning machines and attending to customers, it would be late afternoon before I had a chance to riffle through the Buy & Sell's tools and machinery section, looking at used lathes. They were $150 to $800, depending on condition.

I started calling the sellers of the cheaper machines. Perched behind the counter at Busy Bee, keeping one eye on the front door and one ear out for the hum of the dry-cleaning machine, I'd pick up the receiver of the heavy, black Bakelite telephone, and dial the number.

"Yup, that lathe's gone," one seller answered. "Just sold that baby two hours ago."

I frowned, thanked him, hung up. With the tabloid spread out on the counter, I ran my finger down the column of ads and called the next one.

"Sorry, buddy," came the answer. "I sold it earlier this afternoon."

They couldn't all be sold! I called the next one.

"Yeah, it's gone," he replied. "Guy already picked it up."

I hung up. The hum of the dry-cleaning machine ceased, so I put Buy & Sell aside to empty it. As I hung the warm garments on the rolling rack, an idea began to bloom in my mind. What if I could get to those sellers before everyone else? Perhaps I could buy the machine right away, then sell it the following week for a slightly higher price.

I rolled the full rack over to my co-worker Lena, the young Italian woman who was expert at pressing clothes, and I returned to the counter to wait on customers. But my mind was on lathes. I had two problems: no money, and how to get a copy of Buy & Sell before everyone else.

That evening, I asked Mother to ask Father if I could borrow $500. When Father heard my idea of buying and selling used lathes, he quickly shot down the idea. He was a conservative and cautious person.

Next I tried my oldest brother Akbar, who by this time had emigrated with his wife to Canada. They lived about thirty miles away. Having just moved, he was unable to help. Five hundred dollars in 1975, the equivalent of almost $2,500 in 2020 dollars, was no small amount.

I turned to sister Yasmin, who with her family had now moved from Nairobi to their own place in Vancouver. She said her husband Noordin wouldn't approve any loan to a brother-in-law, but Yasmin had her own savings account. She'd loan the $500 to me for no more than three months, on one condition: don't tell Noordin.

No problem! That was the money problem, solved.

Next I phoned the Buy & Sell office and asked where I could buy a copy the earliest. The receptionist said I could come to their office in Richmond, a suburb of Vancouver, and buy a copy at 10 a.m. Wednesdays.

Wow, I thought as I hung up. A slow smile spread across my face, and I felt a stirring of excitement rising in my belly. *This might work!*

The next Wednesday, I was at the front door of the Buy & Sell office, on the second floor of a dingy commercial building in Richmond, by 9:45 a.m. As soon as they opened the door, I handed them my quarter, took my copy, sprinted down the dark, musty stairwell and jumped into my vehicle, a used, faded-red, hippie Volkswagen van that had replaced my busted Chevy a few months earlier. I sank down in the driver's seat and circled ads for lathes that were in the $150 to $300 range, then drove to the nearest telephone booth (no cell phones back then) and called a seller who'd listed his lathe for $250.

I drove there immediately. The thing was a mess. It looked as if it had had oil mixed with dirt slopped over it regularly. Its bed-ways (the main guides of the machine) were heavily rusted, its crevices were full of tiny metal chips and shavings, and it had almost no original paint left. Lathes in general are considered to be the world's oldest original power tool, and this one looked as if it had been in use from the early days of the Industrial Revolution.

"Looks like you have used this machine a lot!" I said, checking out the crusty machine and pointing out the obvious deficiencies. "I'll pay $150, and I'm taking a risk at that."

We settled at $175. I scribbled out a quick bill of sale and had him sign it as I handed over the cash. During the few minutes it took for me to load the lathe in my van, I heard him behind me, answering his phone over and over, each time saying, "I just sold it."

I felt he might be having second thoughts about selling it so cheap. But I had a bill of sale in my pocket, with his signature.

I drove to the side door of Busy Bee Dry Cleaners and unloaded the lathe, where I had cleared out some room for my purchase so I could store it for a while, if I needed to. It weighed about 200 pounds, but at age 24, I was strong as a bull and that was easy for me. (If I tried to pick that up nowadays--you'd have to dial 911!)

I spent several evenings stripping out the parts and cleaning the machine inside and out. Turns out, the dry-cleaning solvent perchloroethylene, known as perc, is a powerful grease cleaner on metal as well as fabric. When I had the machine nice and clean, I bought $10 worth of gray paint, carefully repainted the lathe body—and suddenly I'd transformed that old soldier into a thing of beauty.

I listed it for $250 in the Buy & Sell, where there was no charge for placing an ad. I may have glorified it by calling it "well looked after," but who could blame me? I certainly had taken good care of it. The first guy that came to see it made an offer immediately, and we soon agreed on $225.

I was thrilled! My entire cash outlay for machine and paint had been $185. I went home that evening and showed my mother the $40 profit I'd made, and she was so happy for me, as she knew I had been struggling. I told Leili, who suggested I give the profit to my mother. I said I would, in due time, but right now I had to make enough to keep buying and selling lathes, plus I needed to repay my sister quickly.

Now I knew my idea could work. I kept on buying and selling used lathes, and within two months, I had converted the initial loan of $500 into $1,200.

It was a sweet day when I drove to Yasmin's home, a month before repayment was due, to give her $507. The $7 was for interest she would have earned over two months. At first, she refused to take the interest, but I insisted. I was happy I could repay her early, before Noordin could find out.

Initially, all I had wanted was a lathe of my own. But now—that could wait! I'd had a taste of capitalism. I was making money. Why would I stop?

CHAPTER 11

Momentum

A s my little side business of buying, fixing, and selling used lathes grew, I quit my two other evening jobs of cleaning carpets and doing alterations at the dry-cleaning store. But I could not focus full-time on lathes. I was still running Busy Bee Dry Cleaners, and since Father had recently purchased another, satellite dry-cleaning location in Richmond, now I also had to drive there every morning, pick up clothes, take them back to Busy Bee to clean, and return them to the Richmond location in the afternoon.

I could not remember ever being so busy! After long days at the store, I'd work late into the nights buying, fixing, and selling used lathes. I was grateful that I could concentrate on my work and grow my business, since Leili was caring for our young son, Shabir, and taking care of all household chores and cooking. She made sure I was eating well, as I worked so hard.

Working on the machinery, I encountered every sort of problem including broken gears, burned-out motors, and stripped threads. Not all the used lathes were as simple to fix as the first one. Heavy rust, busted tool posts, mis-wired switches, bad spindle bearings, and other issues were common. I used every negative point to negotiate a lower price from the seller, and then I got very, very good at fixing machines.

I figured if I were going to do this as a business, I'd have to form a company. I called my company Busy Bee Machine Tools, after the dry-cleaning store (Busy Bee), and incorporated it in British Columbia.

I soon gained a reputation throughout lower B.C. as the guy to call for used lathes, so I started a waiting list of people who wanted lathes.

Sometimes, when I acquired a clean used lathe in good condition, I could sell it that same day by calling one of the customers on the list. I wasn't greedy about the amount of profit. My goal was to sell, sell, and sell some more! The faster I sold them, the more money I could accumulate, and the sooner I could buy more to sell.

Customers began asking me for other machines, such as drill presses, milling machines, metal-cutting bandsaws, and brand-new lathes. Most were unfamiliar, so I took an evening course in machine shop technology and quickly got acquainted with a wide variety of machines and how to use them.

I started contacting wholesalers to buy these items, but they wouldn't sell to me; they wanted me to buy from one of their distributors. I learned how this industry worked: the manufacturer would sell to the importer, who would sell to the distributor, who would sell to a dealer, who would then sell to the end user. Obviously, that became expensive for the consumer, having multiple layers of profit for all the middlemen. No wonder my used lathes were so popular.

Eventually, I connected successfully with an importer of drill presses, milling machines, bandsaws, and new lathes of assorted sizes. This local importer sold directly to dealers. All I needed to provide was a resale certificate, which is a document proving I was a legitimate retailer, and the importer gave me thirty days to pay for the goods. This was very exciting!

I got three drill presses at $140 each. Other dealers were selling these for $200 each. I priced mine at $150, via free ads in Buy & Sell. I didn't care that I'd make only $10 per machine. With 30-day terms from my supplier, I hadn't yet paid anything for them. Since I'd sell before I had to pay, it was all profit without any investment.

I converted a 10-foot-by-10-foot portion of the dry-cleaning store's front lobby into my space for selling machines. I built a simple wall of two-by-fours and added some inexpensive 1/8-inch-thick paneling to close it off from the dry-cleaning counter area. My "retail showroom" contained my desk and a bench on which I displayed a lathe. On the floor across from the bench were one drill press and a small milling machine. It was standing-room-only in my showroom. My company name of Busy Bee Machine Tools was appropriate to prevent confusion for customers who were looking for the machinery company. Customers who came in for dry-cleaning had no idea what was going on behind the new wall. But customers who came in looking for machinery were taken around the counter into my tiny showroom, where their first comment was often "Well, I'll be damned."

The guy who bought my first new drill press offered $146, which I accepted. Only then did he mention he had no way of getting the machine across town to his home.

"No problem," I said cheerfully, happy with the sale. "I'll deliver it after I close the store tonight."

That evening, I drove across town with the new drill press, still in its carton, to the high-end neighborhood of Kerrisdale. I backed my beat-up, faded red VW van into his driveway, got out, and looked around. It was an attractive, upmarket house, and yet he had negotiated with me as if he were a pauper! He hadn't even paid me yet.

I heard the mechanical ratchet of his garage door rolling up, and my customer, a man of about forty, nicely dressed now for dinner, strolled out onto the driveway. "Here's the thing," he said in lieu of a greeting. "I have a bad back, and I'd like you to put the machine on my bench inside the garage."

I was young, but not naive. "Sure," I said. "But I'll need to take payment first."

He paid, so I removed the components from the carton, assembled them, and lifted the 150-pound drill press onto his bench.

I hopped back into my van, waved goodbye to my happy customer, and drove through the tree-lined streets as dusk fell. I was happy that the day's work was over, and I was looking forward to a late dinner at home with

Leili.

I was not thinking this guy had taken advantage of me. Instead, I thought, *I have $6 more in my pocket than I had this morning.*

That $6 profit on my first new drill press would add to my capital that would allow me to buy more machines. That $6 was a push toward success. That evening, I could feel the momentum start to build.

Photo of Old Drill Press

CHAPTER 12

The Dirty Business of Earning a Living

My side business of Busy Bee Machine Tools was exciting, even fun. I loved doing deals! Negotiating, buying, selling—it was a fast-paced game, and it was a thrill to discover I was good at it.

Unfortunately, I still had to earn a regular living, and that meant I was working full-time running Busy Bee Dry Cleaners. Dry-cleaning is by definition a dirty business, and I disliked it: handling soiled clothes, the continual exposure to perchloroethylene (the solvent used in dry-cleaning machines) and the pervasive smell of chemicals. I showered every night as soon as I got home, but Leili constantly complained that my breath smelled of perc.

People bring their clothing to a dry-cleaner for a reason: the clothes are dirty, and in many cases, filthy. I had to receive these at the counter, sort them, tag them, and pre-treat spots, all before putting them in the dry-cleaning machine.

Pre-treating spots is a job in itself, requiring a specialized machine called a spotting table. It looks like a thick ironing board with a grate on one end. The grate allows fluids or cleaning agents to be flushed through a pipe to the sewer below. The machine has one foot-pedal to engage the vacuum, which sucks those fluids down and away. Another foot-pedal forces steam through the steam gun that's handled by an operator, in this case, me.

Most clothing that came in was soiled from ordinary wear. Some items had a stain or a wine or coffee spill. All that was normal. But a small percentage of garments were foul enough to cause extreme disgust. Two examples of the latter remain etched in memory fifty years later.

Ding! The mechanical bell on the store's front door announced a customer. As he entered, I groaned inwardly. He came in nearly every Monday morning, bringing the same sweater tightly wrapped in a plastic bag.

"Good morning!" I said with a cheerfulness I did not feel.

The man was no older than thirty. He had a little potbelly and was starting to lose some hair. He laid several loose garments on the counter and placed the plastic-wrapped sweater on top. "Good morning," he replied, with genuine enthusiasm. He always seemed to enjoy our little Monday-morning encounters.

I did not. Slowly, I opened the plastic bag, holding it out from me, turning my head away. It didn't help. The stench coming off the sweater nearly overwhelmed me; I made a face and tried not to gag.

The sweater was plain beige—I knew this from cleaning it before—but on Monday mornings, it looked like a brown-and-orange print. The front was covered, encrusted really, with dried-on barf. Even worse, you could tell it was pizza-and-beer barf. And it had been sealed in plastic for 24 to 48 hours. The guy obviously couldn't hold his drink.

Crusty Sweater-Man giggled. He always watched my face and seemed to enjoy my expression. He smiled broadly, plucked his receipt off the counter, pivoted on his heel, and exited. The ding of the doorbell announced that our encounter was over.

Except for the work I had to do on that sweater. First, I closed my mind to the weekend bar scene that had resulted in this crusty sweater. I picked up the sweater by the edge of the sleeve and threw it in the dry-cleaning machine by itself, to remove the chunks and most of the smell. I dared not clean it with other garments. When it came out, only then did I tag it, and take it to the spotting table so I could remove the remaining flakes of what must have been a pepperoni pizza. Then I would put it through the dry-cleaning machine again, and it would emerge as its beautiful beige self, without spot or stain or smell.

This customer was always happy when he came to pick up his freshly cleaned clothes, and a happy customer is a repeat customer, so I got to see Crusty regularly.

Crusty came once a week. Crotchman was a monthly customer. He brought in his own and his wife's clothes. It was his wife's white pants that were memorable, with a familiar bloodstain in the crotch. I knew how to take the stain off, but I always wondered, why would a woman wear white pants during those days?

At the spotting table, I applied a fluid of ammonia mixed with another agent. Using a spatula made of bone, I'd work the spotting fluid gently into the stain to loosen the particles. Then I used the steam gun and vacuum to flush the stain off. Once in a while, while aiming the steam gun at the stain, the spray would hit a crease somewhere and ricochet back up at my face. I'd yelp with dismay, drop the steam gun on the table, and run to the bathroom to wash my face with soap and water, over and over.

But when I was done with those white pants, they were pristine. I took pride in hanging the pressed, fresh garment on our little overhead conveyor, all set and waiting for another happy customer to pick them up. And since a happy customer is a repeat customer, I saw Crotchman regularly as well.

It was a dirty business, earning this particular type of a living.

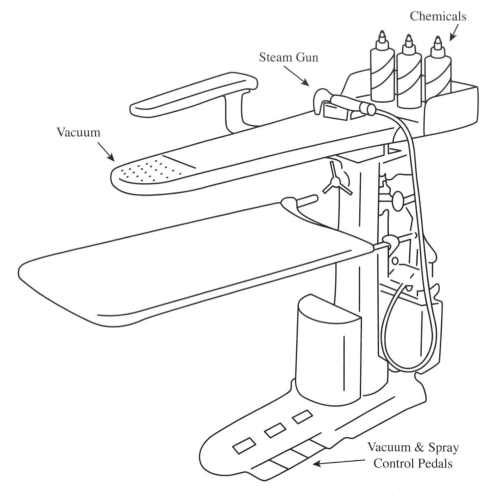

Chemicals

Steam Gun

Vacuum

Vacuum & Spray
Control Pedals

Spotting Table for Removing Stains

CHAPTER 13

No Drill Presses for You!

I was getting busier and busier with my full-time job of running the ever-expanding dry-cleaning business, while my second business of buying and selling lathes, drill presses, and other machinery was ramping up fast. Night after night including weekends, I'd fall into bed exhausted after logging 16-hour days. I would've found irony in the names of both businesses—Busy Bee Dry Cleaners, and Busy Bee Machine Tools—if I hadn't been so tired being a busy bee myself to laugh at it.

By 1977 within Busy Bee Machine Tools, sales of new machinery had eclipsed the profits of the used machinery that I'd been re-building and selling. New machines were easier to sell. Plus, I had less cash outlay up front since my local importer, a congenial guy named David, gave me 30-day terms, and so I made more money, more frequently.

I was thankful to David for giving me the opportunity to buy wholesale from him when none of the other local dealers would sell to me.

On the used-machinery side, inventory was much more limited. There just weren't that many used machines out there, and each one I did get required hours of my time to pick it up, negotiate for it, repair and repaint it.

My first order of new machines in late 1976 had been three drill presses. Now, in early 1977, I was regularly buying ten at a time, because I was pricing them so cheaply compared to other dealers that demand was very high. Ten drill presses were the maximum that would fit in my faded red VW "hippie" van. This particular van had the engine in the back and was not designed to carry that much weight! When loaded with drill presses, my van sometimes scraped the bottom of the road, so I drove slowly. I tortured that poor thing.

One day I called about my order as usual, asking the receptionist if they had them in stock. When she replied they had plenty, I got into my van and headed to the warehouse, pulling around to the loading dock in back to pick them up. The warehouse employee was outdoors, stubbing out a cigarette against the concrete. When he saw me, instead of rolling up the big overhead door so we could load, he said, "Boss wants to see you." He motioned me in through the man-size door back through the warehouse to the office.

Wonder what David wants, I thought as I glanced at my watch. I didn't have any extra time. I walked faster, passing a mountain of stacked drill presses off to the right. It looked as if they'd just received a big shipment. That was good, they wouldn't have any trouble filling my order quickly.

David stood as I entered.

"Shiraz, I want to thank you for the business you've given us, and especially for how quickly you pay your bills," he said, smiling broadly. "You've become our best customer very quickly."

"Thank you!" I replied, smiling and relaxing a little. "It's a pleasure working with you, too."

I waited. He paused. His face grew serious.

"Unfortunately, we don't have any drill presses to sell to you."

I was puzzled. "But I just walked past a whole pile of drill presses. Looks like you just got a shipment in."

"Our other dealers in town are complaining that since you're selling our machines so cheaply, they're unable to compete with you on pricing," David said.

What?! Wouldn't that be their problem, not mine? Didn't David just say I was his best customer? I was speechless.

"Our business relationship has to come to an end," David said.

My mind raced. This could not be! I had to think fast.

"How about one last shipment, just today?" I said. "I have customers waiting for them."

"I'm sorry." David was firm. "But no."

I looked at him for a couple of seconds, then held out my hand to shake his, thanked him for the business we did, and left his office.

My head pounded with panic as I walked back through the warehouse, glancing again at the huge stack of drill presses, which were not available to me anymore. I was instantly out of the new machinery business. Driving back to the dry-cleaning store, I felt shock, but back at work, as the hours passed, I got angry. *How dare they? Why should I be in a situation where someone else controls what I can buy? How can someone else even be in a position to have such an impact on my business?* I'd been grateful for the chance to buy, but now what? My thoughts roiled all that day and through a sleepless night. Without new machinery, I would be sentenced to the dry-cleaning business for life, while fiddling around selling used machinery on the side.

I arose the next day with a new purpose. David's company wasn't making drill presses themselves; they were buying them from some manufacturer overseas. I phoned the local branch of the Canadian customs office to ask what sort of license I'd need to import machinery. They replied that no license was necessary. This was a pleasant surprise; in Africa, a license was required to import anything.

But the bigger problem still loomed. How would I find an importer overseas? I knew the machines I wanted were manufactured in Taiwan, but in 1977, decades before the internet and Google, I had no way to find factories that were half a world away. That information was impossible to get.

Or was it? A single thought rose in my mind. What if I drove around to the various machinery dealers throughout Vancouver and picked up their brochures advertising lathes? Could one of those brochures possibly include the name and address of the factory that manufactured them?

A glimmer of hope began to grow in my mind. As soon as I could get away for an hour from the dry-cleaning business, I hopped in my hippie van and drove to the nearest dealer to get a brochure. It contained only the dealer's contact information, nothing about the manufacturer. Three days passed before I could get to the next dealer, whose brochure was similar. A couple more days went by before I could get to the third. Nothing. My hope was fading, but there were still a couple of big dealers I hadn't visited yet.

Three more days passed, days filled with a steady parade of customers dumping dirty clothes on the counter, days filled with the steam gun and ammonia spot-remover and scraper, days filled with the ever-present cloud of perchloroethylene permeating the air around me. I got back in my van and drove further out, to a large machinery dealer I had not visited yet. I stood in their little reception lobby, scanning the brochure—and there it was, in small type on the back page, at the bottom: the Taiwanese manufacturer's name and address.

In that moment, my destiny changed.

CHAPTER 14

Hippie Van Goes Missing

Being an entrepreneur is like mountain climbing. You're in a valley looking up at a mountain peak, a problem you have to solve. As soon as you solve that problem and scramble over that peak, you see another problem, another peak, before you.

I finally had in hand the contact information for a Taiwanese manufacturer. Now I had to convince them to sell to me.

I wanted to give the impression I was a large, established company accustomed to placing big orders with factories all over the world. Otherwise I likely wouldn't get a response, and certainly I wouldn't get favorable pricing. So, I had letterhead printed with "Busy Bee Machine Tools, Head Office" and the address of the dry-cleaning store. I ordered quality paper, a heavyweight, cream-colored sheet with a linen look to it. It felt good just to hold that letterhead in my hands, feeling the raised ink of my company's name. The recipient didn't need to know the head office of Busy Bee Machine Tools was a 10-foot-by-10-foot space carved out of a dry-cleaning store lobby.

The only way for me to communicate globally in 1977 was via airmail. No internet meant no email, which would not come into common use for another twenty-three years. A large company would have had a Telex machine, an extremely expensive machine that took a typed message, changed it to a series of holes punched in paper tape, transferred it to the overseas recipient's Telex, and changed it back into a readable message.

Of course, I didn't have a Telex. My beautiful letterhead took a week to get there and another week to get back. That's not counting any time it might spend sitting on the recipient's desk. I made sure to ask all my questions in the first letter; I'd better not forget any details, or it would add another two weeks.

Within three weeks, I had received brochures from three different lathe manufacturers in Taiwan! Though I'd only written to one, apparently snitches within a factory would pass on information about potential customers to competing factories.

And the pricing was low! I had recently been buying a 10-inch-by-30-inch lathe from my local importer, David, for $1,900, and selling it for $2,000 (while other local dealers sold it for more than $2,500). Now the Taiwanese manufacturer was offering me this exact item for $900 plus shipping.

I planned to order four, telling the manufacturer my number was small because it was a "trial order." For me, four would be a huge financial stretch, since unlike David who'd offered 30-day terms, I now had to have the money in the bank before I could order the machines.

With shipping, import duty, and tax, my cost for each would be $1,150. I needed to open a Letter of Credit (L/C), which is a document from a bank that guarantees payment. It works like this: my bank would commit to paying the overseas factory's bank; that bank would confirm to the factory that payment was assured via the L/C; the factory would produce and ship the goods and deliver the original set of documents (proof of shipping) from the shipping company to the bank; their bank would pay them and send the documents to my bank; my bank would collect the money from me and hand over the documents. I needed these documents so the shipping company would release the goods to me.

But since I was a new customer, my bank required me to have all that money deposited with them before I could even start the process. I was grateful that I had enough money saved from all my previous buying and selling to pay the bank for the L/C in advance.

Finally, my first overseas order was on the water, chugging toward the port of Vancouver! I had successfully scaled that peak. But before that machinery would ever arrive at my 10-by-10 Head Office in the dry-cleaning lobby, I'd have to deal with several more problems, problems I didn't even know were in store for me.

When I received notice that my shipment had cleared Canadian customs, the following morning I drove to Budget Truck Rental, parked my faded red VW hippie van on the street out front, and rented a 5-ton truck with a liftgate that could accommodate a thousand pounds. I would use the liftgate to lower each 1,000-pound lathe off the truck, then use a four-wheeled-cart to move it into the dry-cleaning store, where I'd cleared the small space for storage.

Driving the big truck, I arrived at the port at 11:30 a.m., where the guard let me drive in through the gate but told me I couldn't pick up anything since the dockworkers were going on strike. Indeed, the place was chaos. I drove slowly toward the rear, where I'd been told my shipment would be. Many times, I stopped because clumps of dockworkers were milling around, some with signs, some chanting slogans, some sitting on crates here and there doing nothing. I rolled my window down to ask questions, but the dockworkers didn't answer, except for one who yelled "We are closed!" As waves of workers marched toward the front security gate, I drove into the almost-empty warehouse, parked the truck, and started looking among the stacked crates for my lathes.

"Hey! You're not allowed in here!" A single dockworker strode slowly toward me. He was at least 60, with a grey, unshaven bristle, but his posture showed strength, as did his tone.

I waved my documents, the bill of lading showing I could pick up my lathes. "I have to get my goods," I said. "I only have the truck for one day. I can't afford to rent it again and come back."

"Doesn't matter," he snapped. He took my bill of lading, his fingernails rimmed with black, the creases in his hands dark with grease that looked as if it would never come off. "I shouldn't even be talking to you," he said, his eyes scanning my document. "Nothing is getting loaded today. We're off the job until we get fair treatment from the port!"

I thought of my lathes sitting somewhere in this warehouse, just out of reach. I thought of the $4,600 I'd given the bank to get them. I thought of my truck rental bill growing larger.

"I'll give you $10 if you help me load my four crates!" I was desperate. "It will only take a few minutes."

He smirked and held out my documents. I didn't take them. He looked at me, saw the desperation in my face, and in that moment, his scowl softened. He glanced back down at the documents.

"Oh, they're right there," he said, motioning to two large crates not ten yards from us.

A thought blipped across my mind: Two crates? Why two, when I'd ordered four lathes? But I didn't want to derail my helper. He glanced around, saw no one, then climbed into a forklift and maneuvered the two crates into my truck.

When I held out a ten-dollar bill, he smiled under his grey bristle. "Keep it, kid," he said, and walked out to join his fellow longshoremen on strike.

By the time I arrived at the dry-cleaning store, it was 4 p.m. I pulled up in the alley near the side door and jumped out, to see what I was up against. The factory had packed the four lathes into two crates. It had never occurred to me to ask about that. Each crate weighed 2,000 pounds, twice what the liftgate could handle. I had no forklift and no one to help. I called Leili and told her why I'd be late tonight. She was worried.

As was I. Up in the truck, I sat alone on one of the crates, thinking. Ten minutes ticked by. I couldn't leave the crates on the truck and figure it out tomorrow; I had to return the truck by early morning to avoid another day's charge.

What was I going to do? Then I thought of the ancient Egyptians building the pyramids. If they can move tons of stone without machines, I certainly can move a couple of thousand pounds on my own.

I got my crowbar and ripped apart the first crate, exposing two lathes, bolted to the bottom of the pallet. I removed the nuts from the bolts so I could lift each end of the machine, one at a time, up and off the boards. I was young, and strong. Using a two-by-four piece of lumber, I scooted the 1,000-pound lathe onto the liftgate, lowered it, maneuvered each end of the lathe onto my steel cart, and rolled it into the dry-cleaning store, once again lifting each end off of the dolly and onto the floor. It was slow and arduous work.

I got home after midnight. Leili was waiting, with dinner and a massage for my aching back.

Next morning, I was able to return my truck within the 24-hour window, but my hippie van was missing. *Stolen?* I thought. *Who would want to steal that piece of garbage?*

In the truck-rental lobby, I learned the city had towed it. No parking on the street between 6 p.m. and 6 a.m., the rental truck receptionist said.

Now they tell me. Insult to injury! I paid the towing company to release my van.

I put an ad in the Buy & Sell, pricing each lathe at $1,250. I priced low because I didn't know how customers would respond, and since I'd prepaid for the machines, I needed to move them fast. But on Wednesday afternoon, when Buy & Sell hit the streets, my phone started ringing and did not stop. By Thursday evening, I'd sold all four.

This was excellent! I told the callers who'd missed out I had another shipment coming. The price would be $1,300, and a nonrefundable deposit paid now would hold a lathe for them as soon as they came in. My $1,300 was still about half of what similar machines were being sold for around town. Within a week, I'd taken deposits for five machines. I opened another L/C at the bank with no problem, placed an order with the factory in Taiwan for ten machines, and two weeks later, had pre-sold all ten.

I had to deal with two more issues before the shipment came in. I needed space to store these machines when they came in, and I needed a forklift to unload them. Wiser now, I had insisted the factory pack each machine in its own crate, as a condition to my order.

Next door to the dry-cleaning store was Frank's Barber Shop, where I got my hair cut. I'd often wondered, as I sat idly while Frank clipped, what was in the rest of the building, closed off behind his two-chair barber shop. Frank said it was mostly empty space, with alley access only.

When I asked, Frank told me he was paying $300 monthly rent for his shop, which included the back space. Would he rent the back area to me for $150 a month? Why yes, he would! I would need to cut a much larger doorway in back, and have a concrete ramp poured to accommodate a small forklift. Though the building was not his, he quickly agreed.

I bought a used forklift for $2,500. This time, when my shipment came into port, I had a trucking company deliver them on a flatbed. I unloaded them with my forklift and stacked them in my back o' the barber-shop warehouse. Every time I fired up the forklift out back, Frank's customers up front got a thrill.

With these problems behind me, my business was picking up speed. I ordered ten more lathes and pre-sold them before they arrived. I found a manufacturer that made drill presses and ordered thirty-five, all of which were sold within a week, at a profit of $15 each. Busy Bee Machine Tools was rolling along, faster and faster.

It was time for me to grow. I needed to connect with more manufacturers. The place to do that would be at a trade show, and I saw there was one coming up, halfway across the world.

The dry cleaning store where Busy Bee Machine Tools was launched by Shiraz in 1975. Customers were taken around the counter into the 10' x 10' "showroom" that had three machines, one on a bench & two on the floor.

A Bad Case of Capitalism

CHAPTER 15

Six Beers and Six Girlfriends

Taipei, Taiwan's capital, would host its first-ever machine tool show in 1977. I had to be there! I bought the cheapest round-trip flight available, at $450, which took me from Vancouver to Anchorage and then Seoul, where I spent the night in a hotel paid for by the airline. I landed in Taipei at 2 a.m., forty-eight hours after leaving Vancouver. (Today, Vancouver to Taipei takes less than thirteen hours.)

At that dark hour in Taipei, with almost no traffic on the roads, taxis would drive by still honking at random, as if it were a reflex action from daytime. I barely heard them; I fell into bed at my hotel and slept like the dead.

The real noise started early next morning: Taipei was a sensory overload of blaring cars, buses, motor scooters and bicycles, plus the occasional cart pulled by a water buffalo. As I made my way to the public hall hosting the show, street vendors offered grilled shrimp, octopus, crisp savory pancakes, chunky tofu. Women held umbrellas against the sun, and a construction worker carried two baskets of bricks via a yoke across his back. Used to the cool, clean air of Vancouver, the steamy pollution of Taipei was a shock.

But not as much as the bathroom within the show hall. The bathroom floor was coated with a layer of urine, drying here and there into sticky pools. The stalls had no toilet paper, and the toilets were just holes in the floor. I had seen these in Africa and was not surprised, but God help a Westerner if he tried to do a big job while balanced in a squatting position and lost his footing on the slippery tile! The sinks had no soap or paper towels, but at least there were sinks. The stench was so overpowering, it made me want

93

to run back to the polluted air outdoors, which in comparison now seemed like fresh mountain air. After one visit to the facilities, I vowed to drink less coffee.

The show itself was nothing fancy, but that didn't matter. I was there to make contacts, and make them I did. One was James Chen.

"Hi! Hi! Where from?" a perky young male voice asked.

It was 4 p.m. on the first day of the show. I was standing by the Chin Yu Chucks company booth, deep in their brochure, packed in among a crowd of show visitors of varied nationalities. I swiveled my head to find the source of the voice. Who had spoken?

"From India?" the voice piped up again.

I glanced around again, then down. A Taiwanese guy about five feet tall, in the Chin Yu Chucks booth, seemed to be addressing me. His eyes were bright, his round face friendly, his thick, shiny black hair parted on one side. I smiled tentatively. He looked like a schoolboy, despite his suit and tie. The suit was loose; he couldn't have weighed more than 110 pounds.

"From India?" he prompted again.

"Shiraz Balolia, Busy Bee Machine Tools," I replied, holding out my hand. "I wrote to your company once, and I got a reply. My father was born in India, but I was born in Africa, and I live in Canada now. Vancouver."

"Vancouver!" the youngster crowed. "Ah, yes, I remember!" As he shook my hand, he rattled off the names of a couple of machinery companies in B.C.

This kid knew his stuff. I put down my brochure, and we began to talk. I was twenty-four and James Chen was eighteen when we met. He was the export manager for Chin Yu Chucks. A chuck is the part that holds the rotating cylindrical workpiece in a metal-cutting lathe. He was smart, a go-getter who'd taught himself English by reading the dictionary. His vocabulary was as impressive as his knowledge of our industry, but his sentence structure was, to put it kindly, extremely creative.

"Ah… my friend, welcome," James said.

I knew that this guy would be a wealth of information about lathe companies in Taiwan, since Chin Yu sold chucks to most of the factories that built and exported lathes. I told him I wanted to see many suppliers, and maybe he could introduce me to some.

"Yes, easy!" James smiled even wider, rubbing his palms together. "For drinks we go now. Beer bar close by. I buy beers." Taking my arm, he steered me out of the hall, out through the berserk traffic along the street, and through a doorway into a shadowy bar that was thick with cigarette smoke and loud with the shouts of salesmen toasting each other.

I disliked beer, but I got through one bottle before switching to Coke. James more than made up for my lack, downing beer after beer as we talked on.

As the evening grew later and my jet lag fiercer, James looked at the six empty bottles in front of him, seeming to notice their number for the first time, and motioned to the waitstaff to bring the bill. He picked it up and hesitated, suddenly looking sheepish. "I need ask big favor. Can I borrow money from you?" He looked at the bill, too embarrassed to tell me he did not have the money to pay for the drinks.

I laughed and reached for my wallet. "No problem, let me get it."

"No, no, you my guest," he said. "You loan me. Only loan. I pay back soon."

I paid, assuring James it was just a loan—but I knew I'd forgive the loan.

The following evening, I was a guest at a hosted dinner, a most useful one since ten local factory bosses were there. During drinks at the table before dinner, I was deep in conversation when a commotion at the door caught my eye. I swiveled my head and saw James making an entrance, escorting not one, not two, but six beautiful young Chinese women, three of them linked elbow to elbow on each side of him. Once again, his eyes were bright, his manners fine, his personality on full power. He had a big smile on his face, and all the girls were giggling.

The men at the table erupted in laughter and a loud torrent of Chinese, which even a non-Chinese speaker like me could tell was some serious ribbing aimed at James.

I was told all six were his girlfriends. When someone asked the girls if that was true, they all nodded, giggling, and fluttered closer around James.

My 1977 trip to Taiwan was the start of not only a long and productive business relationship with James, but of a lifelong friendship that would eventually bring him closer to me than my own brothers.

I returned to Vancouver having increased my personal connections with Taiwanese factory bosses by a factor of ten. I ordered more and more machinery, which arrived at my back o' the barbershop warehouse next to the dry-cleaning store in skeleton crates. Unlike a solid wood crate, a skeleton crate is more open, with just slats of wood protecting the machine inside. Also, because my total orders weren't yet large enough to require an entire shipping container, my machines were shipped LTL (less than a full container load). That meant my skeleton-crated machines traveled loose, in the dungeon of the ship.

When my first shipment of six bench-top milling machines from Taiwan arrived behind the barbershop, I sprinted out to inspect them. A milling machine "mills off" metal, using special cutters to cut slots, produce flat or irregular surfaces, drill holes, or otherwise shape a part. Each machine in its crate stood about four feet tall and weighed about 500 pounds.

They were beautiful. When you've fixed as much beat-up old machinery as I had, you gain an appreciation for the shiny good looks of new ones. I put my hands carefully on the wood slats and leaned in closer for a better look at my dazzling new merchandise.

A gigantic cockroach leapt out. "Ahh!!" I yelped, jumping back. *What the..?* I'd seen big cockroaches in Africa, but never this big. This creature was the size of my index finger. It scuttled into a crack—a big crack—between the pavement and building. *Ugh!* But never mind, it was gone now. I went back to my duties in the dry-cleaning store. I'd uncrate and store the machines after work.

At 6 p.m. sharp that evening, I locked the front door of Busy Bee Dry Cleaners and went back out to the alley with my crowbar to dismantle crates. As I wrenched the first nail out of wood, the bottom of the crate came alive with a battalion of roaches. They jumped, they scuttled, they exploded from the crate in all directions. I think a couple of them flew.

I leapt away, crowbar still dangling from my hand, taking deep breaths. But the job had to be done. One by one, leaping away whenever one jumped out, I uncrated the machines and fork-lifted them into place in the back of the barbershop. I dumped the broken crates and other packing material in a far corner of the parking lot.

The cockroaches, traveling the world in the bellies of container ships, kept arriving with my shipments from Taiwan. Since roaches in that tropical country were originally forest dwellers, they felt right at home in my wood-slat crates in the warm, humid holds of the ships.

I learned to deal with them. If I uncrated a shipment during the week, on Sunday Leili and I would return to the parking lot, gather the discarded crating material, shake each piece to make sure it was roach-free, and stash it in my faded red VW hippie van to take to the dump. Once in a while I'd hear a scream from Leili, followed by a stomp. Sometimes, by the time Sunday rolled around, roaches had departed the slat-pile to create new homes in their newly discovered country. But if the roach infestation was still heavy, I'd start a fire and burn the wood right where it was piled up.

Despite the roaches that rode along, the machines I kept ordering from Taiwan were fueling the growth of my business. As I'd hoped, the contacts I made there helped turbo-charge Busy Bee Machine Tools, and with more suppliers, I could bring in a larger variety of items. The Taiwan show had another, unforeseen result: the fact that I could fund a trip like this on my own attracted attention from another quarter.

News of my newfound success had reached my father.

A Bad Case of Capitalism

CHAPTER 16

Father's Pressure

Work is work, but success is fun. Busy Bee Machine Tools was an incredible amount of work, but also a thrill because I was making money, more money than I had ever seen. I no longer had to worry about making my household budget every month. Every sale, every small profit, delivered a little bit of happiness. Leili was always by my side and knew exactly how well we were doing, but part of the joy was also telling Mother about my success. My healthy business became a source of pride for her.

What I didn't know was that as I was sharing with Mother, she in turn quite naturally talked of my success with Father.

Much had happened for Father in the year since I'd started selling new machines. He had opened several new remote locations of dry-cleaning stores. I was running a couple of them, and my older brother Anil was running a couple. Meanwhile, Leili and I had moved out of low-income housing to a nicer apartment. We'd even taken Shabir to Disneyland in California, driving there twice in my faded red VW hippie van. My sister Yasmin with her husband and children had moved from Vancouver to San Diego, and we visited while we were there.

The day after we returned from our second trip to California, my father called me into his office and told me to take a seat. My discussions with Father were rare and generally meant he wanted to tell me something or give me advice.

"It's time we talked," Father said, leaning back in his old padded leather office chair, rolling a bit on the casters. "How are you doing in your machinery business?"

I relaxed, happy to talk about Busy Bee Machine Tools. "Really well!" I responded. "My new suppliers in Taiwan are delivering great machines, I'm getting good pricing direct from the factories..." I was still talking about deliveries and import regulations when he held up his hand.

"Very good, very good," he said. "But how much money are you making?"

"In just over a year since I started, I've made $40,000," I said proudly.

Father drew in his breath. His eyes widened. He leaned forward in his old chair. "Forty thousand? Profit?"

"Yes," I said simply. In 1978, that was a huge sum of money. By contrast, he was paying me $4800 per year wages for working at his dry-cleaning stores ten hours a day, six days a week.

"I had no idea it was that much," Father said, leaning forward, arms crossed on his desk. "I'm pleased and happy for you, but..." he paused, "if you want to continue in that business, you'll need to take Anil on as an equal partner."

"What?" I was stunned. "This is my business. I started it. I'm 100 percent owner! Why should I take him as a partner?"

"Shiraz," Father said. "Shiraz. In a family, success has to be shared. Once Anil comes on as partner, I can support your business financially so it can grow even further, faster."

I was shocked. "But Anil doesn't know anything about machines!" I said. "He has no knowledge of this industry at all."

"He will learn," Father said. He leaned back once more in the old leather chair. That let me know our meeting was coming to an end. "Ask Anil to come and help you in your business, and you might see this could be a good thing."

I left Father's office that day feeling totally dejected. But it was an "order" from father whom I had never disobeyed before, so I was willing to give Anil a shot. I asked Anil to come to the back of the barbershop Sunday afternoon and give me a hand moving and fixing machines for a few hours.

That day confirmed my feeling. Though Anil worked hard, he was nowhere near as mechanically inclined as I was. His engineering degree was in electrical design. That didn't help here, where mechanical aptitude, plus hands-on experience fixing machines, was much more important. Bottom line, I had worked hard to build my business and didn't need or want anyone else as a partner. I got the feeling Anil didn't want to be there either, especially on a Sunday when he could be home with his wife and infant son.

The following week, I went back and told Father as much. I told him I did not need any help and would not be taking on any partners.

"Then you have a difficult decision to make," Father said, once again leaning forward over his desk toward me.

My relationship with my Father was such that I could not argue with him. From his tone I knew there was no room for discussion.

He was entirely right about one thing. I had a difficult decision to make, and I made it. Within a couple of months, I started shutting down Busy Bee Machine Tools and prepared to move. It took a lot of guts to shut down my baby when it was making me so much money. Leili and I packed up everything we wanted from our apartment and loaded it onto a trailer. I had recently sold my faded red VW hippie van, so with Shabir on Leili's lap in my new-to-us 1977 Scout II 4-wheel-drive vehicle, we drove to San Diego.

My goal in California was to re-create my work in Vancouver. I bought a small dry-cleaning store in El Cajon, a suburb of San Diego, spending $26,000 of my savings on it. I certainly knew the dry-cleaning business, and as owner, that store would provide a steady income. Meanwhile, I'd start importing machines on a small scale, get a feel for the market, and expand as soon as I could.

Unlike life in Vancouver, in San Diego I had time on my hands, and

I spent some of it upgrading my Scout, a vehicle similar to a Jeep. Working on my Scout, I discovered Dick Cepek's company (today Dick Cepek Tires & Wheels) a Los Angeles outfit that sold aftermarket parts for off-roaders direct to the consumer. I ordered a skid-plate kit (a steel plate that protects the underside of an off-road vehicle) and it arrived next day via UPS.

The company's mail-order catalog was tucked into the carton, and as I flipped through it, all sorts of appealing products beckoned. I set the skid plate kit aside, made myself a big sandwich, and took catalog and sandwich over to my favorite recliner in our new apartment's little living room. As I munched my sandwich, I immersed myself in the fabulous gear in the catalog. Oversize wheels, custom roll bars, lift kits, night lights for off-roading, heavy shocks for off-road racing, custom roof racks, grill guards—for a machinery guy like me, this catalog was like heaven. I read it through once, then twice. By the third time through it, I knew this was the way to sell products. I wanted to come out with a catalog like this for my machinery!

Soon my first shipment of a lathe and a milling machine from Taiwan arrived in San Diego. I sold it within a week or so for a couple of hundred dollars' profit. But there was no flurry of activity on my ads here, as there had been in Vancouver. Importing into the United States was easier than importing into Canada; many companies had already been importing and selling at low prices.

Never afraid of competition, I jumped in and started swinging. I knew my pricing would have to be sharp, and my marketing aggressive.

About this time, I also got aggressive about losing weight. I'd been overweight for years, though in school I played a lot of sports that had kept me from turning into a total potato. But adult life with no time for sports had promoted steady gain, and by the time we moved to San Diego, I weighed 240 pounds. Leili never complained about my weight, but she did say she'd help me try to reduce it. We saw an ad on television for a weight-loss protein powder, with glowing reviews and convincing testimonials, and ordered it.

It came with a booklet that dictated what I could and could not eat. I quickly discovered the powder itself was worthless. Disgusted by the scam, I ditched the powder but followed the booklet, eating basically just a grilled steak and slice of watermelon every single day. No bread, no burgers, no baked goods, no rice. Dark memories of Mr. Shamash and the Congo floated through my mind. No sugar, no juice, no coffee, no fried foods. As per the booklet, I started drinking two to three gallons of water daily.

It was torture, but I was losing weight, and that motivated me.

We liked California generally, but it was hot, especially in El Cajon, and we missed our families. All of Leili's family was in Vancouver now, and all of my family too, except my sister. While we didn't miss the daily drama of family living close by, being this far away made us feel the void.

One day, out of the blue, Akbar called me and said he and Anil would come to San Diego for a few days' holiday. It made sense, because they could visit sister Yasmin as well—but soon after they arrived, their agenda became clear. They'd been talking with Father, and together had come up with the idea of a family business consisting of dry-cleaning stores and machinery sales. At that time, the dry-cleaning stores were fully owned by Father, though we would inherit after he passed. But with this idea of a new corporation, each of us three brothers plus Father would own 25 percent from the start. Father would finance growth in both the machinery and dry-cleaning businesses, and I'd have a free hand running the machinery part. The offer sounded good, and I could return to a market I knew well.

Just a few months after arriving, Leili and I once again packed up, gave notice on our apartment, sold the dry-cleaning store and headed back to the cool, clean air of Vancouver.

And back to the drama of family.

A Bad Case of Capitalism

CHAPTER 17

Back to Canada

"What happened to my son?" Mother cried when she saw me. A smile lit up my face as I gave my mother a great bear hug. Only my hug wasn't as big as it used to be, because I had lost 70 pounds while living in California. I'd also grown a mustache.

"Ask her!" I said, pointing at Leili. "Leili's been in charge of my weight loss program all these months. And she's not as bad as Mr. Shamash in the Congo. Remember him?" We all laughed. It was cold that day in January 1979 when we got back to Vancouver, yet my mother had rushed outside to greet us.

Mother swept up Shabir, and I hugged them both at once. How I'd missed her!

But the larger family's joy upon my return wasn't as deep and long-lasting as Mother's. We three brothers and Father started meeting every evening right away to plan our new business. We held the meetings in my parents' home, in an upstairs bedroom Father had converted to his office.

I got along great with oldest brother Akbar, but early on, it became clear there was bad blood between Akbar and Anil that I hadn't been aware of. I soon realized there was trouble simmering under the surface between Akbar and Father, too.

After the first few evening meetings, our "business" discussions grew heated. Conversation veered toward hashing out old issues and opening old wounds rather than talking about new ideas. Repeatedly, I tried to bring the discussion back to our plans, rather than the dirty laundry that had nothing to do with me.

After the third night of hot tempers, Akbar walked out, saying he wanted no part of the partnership. I ran after him, catching up with him halfway down the stairs.

"Akbar, don't go!" I grabbed his sleeve. "These issues are temporary, they won't last, soon we'll each be busy running different parts of our company. Don't give up!"

"I don't need it!" Akbar snapped. "I don't need this stress in my life! You have no idea what's happened in the past." He continued down the stairs, and in a moment, he was gone from the house.

I tramped slowly back upstairs to Anil and Father, both of them now sitting silent in his office. "Now what?" I asked.

Father gave Akbar a few days to cool off before asking him to reconsider. But at our next evening meeting, it was just Anil, me, and Father gathered around his desk. Father told us our new company would now be the three of us. Akbar was gone forever from the family business.

I was deeply disappointed even though I now held one-third ownership rather than one-fourth. With Akbar's departure, I'd lost an ally. Anil was my father's favorite son. They had a bond that I never understood.

We moved on with the job of creating our business. I named my machinery part of our company Busy Bee Machine Tools, a Division of Busy Bee Imports Ltd., (continuing the name Busy Bee Machine Tools that I had started a couple years prior). Father approached shopping malls around greater Vancouver and quickly secured ten satellite dry-cleaning locations. The original Busy Bee Dry Cleaners on Victoria Street became part of the new company.

The idea was to have a central dry-cleaning location big enough to process clothes from all the satellite drop-off and pick-up locations. We bought a 5,000-square-foot warehouse in the suburb of Burnaby and cordoned off more than half of it for machine storage and showroom. No longer would my machinery customers have to come into a 10-foot-by-10-foot plywood-and-paneling cubby-hole! I also upgraded to a decent forklift.

For the dry-cleaning area within the warehouse, Father bought a used screw-conveyor system to move hanging clothes throughout the space. This 70-foot-long conveyor was basically a 1-inch-diameter screw that turned continuously and was driven by a motor at one end. It worked like this: when clothes came out of the dry-cleaning machine, they'd be hung on the continuously turning screw, travel through a steam chamber, and then move towards the pressers who would take them down, iron each garment, and hang them back on the turning screw. The clothes would continue to the front of the warehouse, where an employee would sort and bag them.

Except Father could not find anyone to install his used conveyor. This screw conveyor could not have posts from the ground supporting the conveyor. It had to be hung from the ceiling, and the ceiling in this warehouse was twenty feet high. No one would touch the project. He called several dry-cleaning machinery dealers. All said it wasn't possible to hang this conveyor from this high ceiling.

I told Father I could do it.

I bought an arc-welding machine that had thirty feet of welding cables. I bought several 20-foot rods of ½-inch rebar. I bought a very tall ladder. I took it all to our empty warehouse and got started.

I placed the ladder against the steel girders twenty feet high that held up the ceiling of the warehouse, then leaned the long rebar rods up against it, where I'd be able to reach them later.

I wrapped the heavy welding cables around my waist and held the handle of the live welding rod, electric current running, in my right hand. I slowly climbed the ladder, grabbing each rung with my left hand. I picked up one 20-foot-long rod of rebar and carefully welded it to one of the metal girders.

The welding was difficult because the fumes gathered up there in the ceiling. I held my breath for fifteen seconds while I was welding, then took five steps down the ladder away from the fumes, to take a deep breath before ascending again to finish the weld. Working carefully, moving the ladder after each one, I welded rebar at 10-foot intervals to the metal girder that held up the screw conveyor.

Looking back, I see the danger. I could've passed out from the fumes and fallen twenty feet to the concrete floor below. I could have been electrocuted, had the two ends of the welding cables touched. I was alone, so if disaster struck, there was no help. Fortunately, none of that happened, and I successfully completed the installation.

But tragedy struck elsewhere in our family. While we were working to launch the business, Mother was diagnosed with stomach cancer and went into the hospital. Always, one of us stayed with her. Yasmin usually spent the night next to her bed, Father came in the morning, and Anil, Akbar, or I came after that. The chemotherapy made her hair fall out. She realized she would not live much longer.

She came home for a few days. She directed that her jewelry be wrapped in bundles and labeled with the name of who was to receive them. As I looked at her sitting next to Father, one of her hands clasped in both of his, I imagined the girl she had been in Mwanza, Tanzania, the girl who'd boldly passed a note through the window of her family home to the handsome young man walking by on his way to work. She'd been fourteen when they married. She was still young now, only fifty-two.

Her home visit was short. She quickly returned to the hospital, and one evening when I arrived for my evening "shift" with her, I found she'd passed away moments before.

She died in May 1979, one month after diagnosis, and four months since we'd returned from California and she'd greeted me with the joyous cry "What happened to my son?"

Leili was pregnant then, and she had a miscarriage a few days after my mother died.

Those were hard days.

Father moved in with Anil, who lived five minutes away from our new Burnaby location. We continued working to get both the machinery and dry-cleaning parts of our business open. We ordered new dry-cleaning and pressing equipment, including a 16-foot-tall steaming press for long drapes. My first shipment of machines came from Taiwan, and I placed ads in the Buy & Sell.

It took a long while before my heart was fully back in it.

A Bad Case of Capitalism

CHAPTER 18

Branching Out into Woodworking Machinery

The machinery side of our business took off like a rocket. I had more resources now to place larger orders for a wider variety of machinery. Also, having learned of the power of catalog marketing in California, I was creating the first catalog.

I had some experience as a photographer. Years before in Nairobi, after school I had photographed weddings as a side business for extra money. Now I purchased professional photography equipment and set up a photography studio in a back corner of our Burnaby warehouse. During any slow moment, I'd run back to that corner to take photos. I photographed every tool and every piece of machinery, I wrote every word in that fifty-page catalog, and in late 1980, I published the first-ever machinery catalog in Canada. Interior photos were black-and-white, but the cover was full color.

I was justifiably proud of the catalog, though today even a cell phone takes better photos than the professional equipment of those days.

In our new company, I tended the machinery side and Anil tended the dry-cleaning. Father did the accounting for both. Since he lived with Anil now, they'd go home for lunch together daily, and I'd cover the dry-cleaning business while they were out. I often worked until 10 p.m., and as late as 1:30 a.m. if I were readying machines for shipping next day. On Saturdays, Anil would help in the machinery showroom, but as Father had promised, I pretty much ran the machinery business with autonomy.

A lot of the fun in this business was chatting with customers about the tools they sought and the projects they used them for. One day, a customer asked me for a planer, to be used for a woodworking project.

I had no idea what he meant. "A planer," I repeated. "Do you mean that hand-held tool for shaving wood?" I thought he was asking for one of those things with a blade at the bottom that you pushed over a slab of wood to remove material.

He laughed and told me a planer is a large power tool with a motor that reduces the thickness of wood, whether that was a massive slab or a simple board. He even had a photo to show me what he wanted. It didn't mean much to me, as I had never sold woodworking machines.

I couldn't help him that day, but now I wanted to know more about it. I took an evening course in woodworking at the local community college, and I discovered woodworking machinery was simpler than metalworking machinery. In general, the craft of woodworking is easier, too. After years of the grinding work of fixing old and balky metalworking machines and dealing with dozens of parts on a single machine, I thought, *Woodworking is easy, this is nothing!*

Shortly after that, another customer asked if I'd heard of Delta. Delta Machinery was the largest manufacturer of woodworking equipment in the United States then, with a distribution center in Toronto that serviced all of Canada. Yes, I answered, I certainly had heard of them. To myself I remembered, *Delta refused to sell to me when I was starting out, saying they had enough dealers in Vancouver.*

Delta had just introduced a new 13-inch planer, made in Brazil. It had hit the market just that week, selling at $1500. Delta at this time was starting to close its U.S. manufacturing due to high labor costs, and instead setting up manufacturing outside the country where labor was cheap and there were no labor laws and unions to worry about.

Paybacks are great! I immediately bought one of the new planers and air-freighted it to James in Taiwan. By now, James and I were working together regularly. I had even previously bought a $2,000 Telex so we could communicate faster. But Telexes from James were devilishly hard to read. His vocabulary was fine, since he'd learned English by reading the dictionary, but his sentence structure was impossible. I had to study his message, mentally shifting the words around until it made sense.

James had a friend in Taiwan who was just starting in machine manufacturing. He took my Delta planer from James and reverse-engineered it (taking it apart, duplicating each part, and reassembling the new parts). Three months after I'd airfreighted it to James, I received at Busy Bee a planer that was identical to the one I'd sent. And my cost was…$350!

I placed an ad in Buy & Sell for it at $550, and people started pouring into our showroom to see it. I couldn't sell my display sample, but I took orders for future delivery. Demand was so brisk that I ordered an entire container of these planers for my first shipment.

Sales of woodworking machinery, like our metalworking machinery, took off! We introduced jointers, table saws, and bandsaws, since I now knew how to use them and what to look for. Father, ever the accountant, noticed the machinery business was booming while the dry-cleaning side was much more laborious and didn't make nearly as much money. We made a collective decision to close the dry-cleaning side, sell the satellite stores, and concentrate on machinery.

Once our central dry-cleaning plant closed, I had to climb that tall ladder once again. This time I went up with an angle grinder, to grind off that rebar and demolish the hanging frame I had so laboriously welded on at my peril two years earlier.

With all three of us now in the machinery business full-time, the first couple of months were a learning process for Anil and Father. I was grateful for Anil's help, especially since it was time for me to take another trip to Taiwan, to attend the machinery show and visit factories in Taichung where manufacturing took place. Leili came with me, sometimes visiting factories with me, sometimes being taken for sightseeing tours by the wives of factory owners.

Once again, my visit to Taiwan turbo-charged business back home.

We started importing machines by the container-load. Over in Taiwan, James would mix-and-match products from several manufacturers, so my order could fill a container entirely. When a full container arrived at Busy Bee Machine Tools in Burnaby, I was usually the one unloading it with a forklift.

The problem was that our warehouse didn't have a dock-high door, so I couldn't drive the forklift directly from warehouse into container and vice versa. The first stack of machines closest to the end near the container's door was easy enough to unload with the forklift. It was the crates farther back that were a nightmare. I rigged up systems using chains, blocks, and straps so I could drag them forward with the forklift before lowering them to the ground.

This involved me jumping up into the container about thirty times, because pallets would often catch on a nail protruding from the container floor, and I'd have to jump back up with a prybar to free it before continuing to drag it.

Late one afternoon, already beat from the day's work, I was unloading a container of double-stacked small milling machines. I had jumped up into the container twenty times already to free stuck pallets. I was down to the last row of crated machines, using a canvas strap, block and tackle attached to the pallets, when it got stuck once again.

I was so tired. I did not want to get off the forklift, jump back up into the container, and pry the crates free. If I continued pulling steadily with the forklift, it would free itself.

I pressed the throttle. I heard the forklift whine. I heard a snap! as the bottom board of the pallet broke. The milling machine, all 600 pounds of it, flew out of the container and landed on the ground between the forklift and the container in a twisted, crumpled pile of crushed and broken metal castings.

I got off the forklift and looked at the machinery laying on the ground. *Well,* I thought wearily, *here's the start of our parts department.*

Old Telex Machine

Photo of Busy Bee in Burnaby

A Bad Case of Capitalism

CHAPTER 19

Something Smells Fishy

Despite the wonky sentence structure in his Telexes, my relationship with James grew stronger by the day. He wanted to launch his own trading company to better serve my business, but he had no money to do so.

I offered him a personal loan to get started. In a way, it was an echo of our first meeting a couple of years earlier, when he had no money to pay the bar bill and asked me for a loan to cover it. Only this time, I asked that he pay me back within one year, and also offer favorable pricing on future machinery sales to me.

It was a handshake deal based on mutual trust, with no documentation or signature or anything showing that I had loaned him money. I'd worked closely enough with James that I felt good about the loan, which indeed would turn out to pay huge dividends in the future.

Meanwhile, closer to home, things were getting shaky. My father and Anil and I regularly met on Wednesdays to discuss strategy and other issues. I noticed a trend: whenever we had to vote on a decision, the vote would land with their two against my one. It occurred to me that since my father was living with Anil, they would naturally discuss things and wind up deciding the issue before the meeting. Any input I had was too late, and my vote was useless. I also noticed that when Anil was by himself with me, he was more reasonable to deal with, but he never went against our father's wishes.

A recurring problem was that neither of them liked James. They thought James was making money off us, and why couldn't we go directly to the manufacturer? I explained that yes, we could do that, but we wouldn't get a better price because James, being Chinese, could negotiate better with a local Chinese factory owner than we could. Also, I never accepted the first price offered, and always sent James back to negotiate a better price with the factories. The price we'd pay for a planer would be the same or even higher if we dealt direct. Plus, James gave us the advantage of procuring product from small factories that we didn't know existed, or whose owners did not speak English. Overall, James was very much worth the 5 percent commission he earned.

Our Wednesday meetings grew more and more frustrating. I told them that since they routinely made decisions beforehand, our meetings were a farce. In business, Father had always been conservative, whereas I was more of a risk-taker. Since Anil would not vote against Father, the vote routinely went Father's way.

I started keeping to myself at work, burying myself in my tasks, avoiding family politics, and venting in private to Leili after work every Wednesday. The joy I had had in working with my hands fixing machines, and buying and selling them, was fading. I had agreed to go into this business with family members because I'd been told I would have total autonomy on the machinery side. Instead the business had evolved to Father effectively making all major decisions. The situation grew steadily worse, until I was avoiding Father almost entirely, keeping any discussion between us to a minimum.

Of course, Father noticed, and asked several times if anything was wrong. It was time for me to leave. But go where?

Years before, my shooting partner Wolf and I, with our wives and children, would regularly drive from Vancouver south across the border into the U.S., passing through the small city of Bellingham in northwest Washington state. Our destination on those trips was a gun shop farther south of Bellingham. I had graduated to a Smith & Wesson 44 Magnum pistol by then, and Wolf had shown me how to cast bullets using discarded wheel weights. I would get a bucket of these from tire repair shops, melt the weights in a casting machine, remove any dirt, then use a mold to cast them as bullets. The bullet is just the tip that flies out of the gun; making them myself was a thrifty solution since I could re-use the brass casing several times. But even with homemade bullets, every couple of months we still needed to drive to the gun shop to purchase supplies such as gun powder, primers, and casings. These things were absurdly expensive in Vancouver.

On the drive home from the gun shop, we'd stop in Bellingham for a bite to eat. Leili and I had often remarked how much we liked the small-town atmosphere there.

Now, as Leili and I talked about a plan for leaving Vancouver, Bellingham came up as an option. Leili was close to her parents and five siblings, all of whom lived in Vancouver, and she didn't want to move too far away. Bellingham was 30,000 people then, and less than an hour's drive from Vancouver. It would be close enough to visit family whenever we wanted. We chose Bellingham as the place for our home and our business.

I talked to Father, who was concerned that I would compete with them if I left. I assured him I had no interest in doing that. I was moving to the United States to live and do business and I would not sell into Canada. I asked him to buy my one-third ownership in Busy Bee Machine Tools. He and I came to an agreement on a price for my shares in the family business, for which he would pay over time.

I hired a high-profile Seattle immigration lawyer to help me make my best presentation to American immigration authorities, and in early 1983, I started my business in USA!

I chose the name Grizzly Imports for my new American-based business. A grizzly bear is a powerful animal, unafraid of anything in the forest. Plus, Grizzly would look great on machines and would be easy to remember.

My bear now needed a home, so I started looking at warehouses in Bellingham. I wanted about 15,000 square feet, with loading dock doors where I could drive the forklift directly into shipping containers.

In February 1983, my realtor and I stood in a 30,000-square-foot warehouse on Meridian Street in Bellingham, sniffing. The smell of fish was overpowering, since the owner was currently renting 5,000 square feet of it to a fish-processing operation.

Greg, the warehouse owner, came out of his small office in the rear of the building next to the fish area, to accompany us for the showing.

After pleasantries, I spoke up. Someone had to.

"This place reeks of fish," I told Greg. "I can't run my machinery business in a warehouse that smells of fish."

Greg's brow furrowed. He sniffed too.

"I don't smell fish at all," he declared. He sniffed again, turning his head this way and that. "Nope, nothing." His eyes narrowed. His brow furrowed deeper. "You're making this up because you see the fish processor back there, and you're trying to get the rent down."

"I'm not making it up!" I said. "With this smell, I wouldn't rent here at any price. If you want to rent 15,000 square feet to me, you'll have to have the fish processor move out."

Negotiations stalled until Greg said he would ask his attorney to come over, to act as a sort of fish-smell judge. "If my attorney says this place smells of fish, I'll give notice to the fish-processing guys," Greg said. "They're on a month-to-month lease for the fishing season, which is just about over anyway."

Fifteen minutes later, Greg's attorney arrived, wearing a nice suit and tie. But he didn't get very far. A few steps into the warehouse, the attorney ran back outside, saying, "Greg, how can you work in this? It smells like a fish market. Now my suit is going to smell of fish!"

That was it. Thirty days later, the fish guys were out, and I had secured the warehouse. Greg built a wall to separate my 15,000 square feet from the rest of the area.

You could say that the bear had won against the fish.

Greg, by the way, was telling the truth. He'd become so acclimated to the fish, he no longer smelled it at all.

Photo of "fishy" Meridian St. Warehouse

A Bad Case of Capitalism

CHAPTER 20

The Bear Comes to Life

The warehouse in Bellingham, now free of fish, was bare-bones space. I needed to have offices built in it and couldn't use the facility until that was accomplished. I was able to convince Greg to give me a month at no charge, so I could get offices built.

During these first months of 1983, I was going back and forth between Vancouver and Bellingham. In Vancouver next to Father's house, a house was being built by two Punjabi Sikhs, one of whom called the other Paaji, meaning older brother. I asked the brothers if they would come help me build three connected offices within my new location across the border. They agreed. I worked alongside them, and the three of us completed the offices in two weeks in April 1983.

When the offices were done, they offered me a partnership in their home-building business, but I was launching this new adventure in the United States and wasn't interested in returning to Vancouver to build houses. Still, I was gratified that they thought so highly of my work.

I had found the warehouse in February, incorporated Grizzly Imports in the state of Washington in March, and built the offices in April. Now I needed to order a computer system that could handle orders and invoicing on a large scale.

I made a list of what I thought the computer should be able to do. Of course, I wrote the list in longhand. In 1983, there were no personal computers, only large systems.

I visited the IBM office in Bellingham, list in hand. The IBM System/34 was the smallest computer that could handle the job. It cost $32,000, but

IBM had a lease program for $600 per month. Delivery was scheduled for June.

There was still much to be done. I had to negotiate orders for all the machines, prepare a catalog, place ads in magazines, and most urgent, find someone who knew how to manage that System/34. Some in the computer industry called the System/34 a mini-computer, but keep in mind, that was in comparison to room-filling mainframes. The System/34 was bigger than a large washer and dryer put together.

I placed a Help Wanted ad in the Bellingham Herald and hired Shirley Olsen, my first employee. She knew the System/34 inside out and agreed to start at the end of June after the system was delivered.

Next, I started planning another trip to Taiwan. I wanted to place new orders, and have proper photographs taken for my new catalog, which I would print in Taiwan to save costs.

This was a perfect opportunity for Leili, Shabir, and I to make that trip into a business vacation. We had not had a vacation in years, except for two road-trips to Disneyland in my faded red VW hippie van. Plus, within the last five years, we had moved three times, started and then sold a business in California, and started and then departed a family business in Vancouver. Time for a break!

In May 1983, we flew from Vancouver to Taiwan, where I negotiated prices and placed orders, then traveled to Osaka and Tokyo before going to Hong Kong, Bangkok, Singapore, and back to Taiwan. Besides enjoying quality time with my family, during that trip I accomplished much for Grizzly.

Most significantly, the trust I had placed in James, when I had loaned him money without any documentation, so he could start his own business, was about to pay off big. Through James, I now secured ninety-day payment terms for all my shipments from Taiwan for the first two years of business. This meant I didn't have any cash outlay for any of the machines I'd be getting from Taiwan until ninety days after I'd received the machines.

That allowed me to really cut down the selling price of the machines and increase the-selection of machines I could sell, without worrying about any lines of credit from a bank. It was the boost I needed to start Grizzly.

The bear had been born!

I had never owned a computer, but I made lists of what I wanted the computer to be able to do. My lofty goals back then were for the computer to be able to process 500-700 orders per day.

Shirley - Grizzly's first employee

System/34 Computer

A Bad Case of Capitalism

CHAPTER 21

The Hell's Angel

"No way!" I said into the phone. I was standing in my office in Grizzly's warehouse on Meridian Street on a warm July day in 1983. The IBM System/34 was now in place and Shirley was working on it so she could process orders as soon as we had sales.

I hadn't stopped to sit down when I answered the phone. I had been running, literally, as I worked at all the tasks necessary to set up the business. I had ads coming out in two weeks, and my first two container shipments of machinery would arrive in a week's time. I expected the containers to come on separate days, and I would unload them myself.

Except that the agent from the shipping company, on the phone, was now telling me the two containers would arrive at Grizzly's loading dock tomorrow morning, and I'd have three hours to get both of them unloaded. Any longer would be charged by the hour.

"No way!" I repeated, but I knew it was probably a lost cause. The containers would arrive at my warehouse loading dock with less than twenty-four hours' notice. I begged the agent to reconsider.

"I need time," I said. "Let's find another option."

"There are no other options," the agent said. "Expect both containers sometime between 8 and 11 a.m., at which point the clock starts ticking."

Dock space at our new warehouse was not a problem. The physical set-up could accommodate several containers at once. The problem was, I could not. No single human being, even someone as young and strong as I was, could unload two full shipping containers of heavy machinery with many small cases that had to be hand-stacked onto pallets within three hours.

I liked doing things myself, and I didn't mind physical labor. But this situation called for help. I got back on the phone and called an agency in town that offered temporary employees, for a day or even a few hours.

"Send me someone who has experience unloading shipping containers," I said. "I need that person here at 8 a.m. tomorrow. Send someone strong!"

Next morning, I was at my desk early when I felt the earth shake and heard a roar of a motorcycle outside the front entrance to the warehouse. I looked at my watch. It was only 7:45, a little early for my helper. The roar of the motorcycle revved again and then fell silent.

I glanced out the front showroom window. I saw a burly guy with dark blond hair that hung in a tangle past his shoulders. A blue bandanna was tied around the top of his head. I could see tattoos on his neck. He swung his leg off the massive hog that was his motorcycle. He looked at the paper in his hand, then at the warehouse address above the door. He was big, 6'3" at least, wearing leather chaps and a leather jacket with some sort of insignia.

Oh God, a gang member? They sent me a gang member?

The door opened, and Gerry St. Laurent walked in.

"Manpower sent me," he said. "You had a couple containers to unload?" He looked around. "Where are they?"

The containers hadn't arrived yet. They could be here within fifteen minutes, or within two hours. I looked at Gerry's bulk, his strong jaw, his don't-mess-with-me gaze. I had not expected to have to deal with someone like this but turning him away might have been hazardous to my health.

"They should be here any minute!" I blurted.

He paused, looking around. The three built-in offices were clean and new, but my concrete-walled warehouse space beyond that showed a smattering of dead leaves, bits of paper, and other debris scattered across the expanse of floor.

"Got a broom?" he asked.

I fetched the 4-foot-wide broom I'd bought a couple of days earlier. Gerry went to the far back corner of the warehouse and started pushing it in a straight line along the back edge, sweeping his way methodically to the front of the warehouse.

I could see this guy wasn't going to sit around waiting for containers to arrive. He hadn't needed to be told what to do, either. I left him to his sweeping and returned to the pile of paperwork on my desk.

Two hours later, after Gerry had swept the entire warehouse and more, the containers finally showed up. We worked side by side; I ran the forklift and Gerry unloaded items onto pallets. He was strong and fast and experienced.

The two drivers who'd delivered the containers watched us work. "You guys are good," one said to us. "How long you two been a team?" Later, they told us they hadn't expected us to get done within three hours.

When the job was done and the containers gone, Gerry and I sat on the loading dock and talked. I asked him why he was working for a temp agency. Gerry said he'd lived in the Bellingham area a couple of years ago and more recently had been passing through, headed to Canada, but had been turned back at the border because he had only $30 in his pocket.

"I figured I'd come back to Bellingham, earn a few bucks, and try for Canada again," he said.

"Are you looking for a full-time job up there?"

"Nah, I want to spend the summer in Canada riding my Harley," Gerry said. He paused and looked at me again. "Why? You offering a full-time job? Because if you are, I could hang around for a while."

Gerry came to work for Grizzly Imports as a full-time warehouse employee at $7 an hour. He was mechanically inclined, and before long could assemble any of the machines that came in. The two of us built the partition wall that created the showroom. (It looked great, but our showroom, like the whole building, felt like an icebox in the winter since the warehouse had no insulation. Working in the showroom during those months meant you had to dress as if you were outside.)

When my magazine ads were published, the phone started ringing. In those days, I charged only for freight shipments, and shipped small parcels free (Amazon—I was way ahead of you). I took customer calls, Shirley processed invoices on the IBM, Gerry packed small items for delivery, and I processed machinery orders. Business was brisk because I set prices low. I wanted to make an impact on this market. Containers arrived steadily, and when they did, Gerry and I worked together to unload everything.

Gerry, who'd initially offered to "hang around Bellingham for a while," stayed with Grizzly for six years, eventually becoming the warehouse manager with many men working under him. It wasn't until years later that I found out he actually had been at one time a member of the notorious Bandidos outlaw motorcycle gang, an international organization with 2,500 members. Gerry hadn't liked that lifestyle, so he left to make his own path in life.

I was lucky, that day in July 1983 when his Harley roared up to the warehouse, that his path intersected with mine.

Big Gerry with Shiraz

CHAPTER 22

The Mail Order Business

I launched my company with the best prices on metalworking and woodworking machinery anywhere in the United States. But that makes no difference unless your market knows it. In 1983, the only way they could know it was via my catalog and ads in magazines. (Internet shopping wouldn't come along for another fifteen to twenty years, and it would take much longer to come into common use.) Throughout most of the 20th century, unless you walked into a store to buy, mail order shopping was king!

The dominant mail order catalog then was Sears Roebuck and Co., which reigned as the largest retailer in the country for most of the century. Their behemoth of a catalog landed in millions of American mailboxes. Other large retailers such as L.L. Bean also acclimatized shoppers to mail order. Catalogs included an order form, which customers would fill out and mail in, and eventually your package would arrive at your door. It was called mail order even after toll-free phone numbers were added.

When I launched Grizzly Imports in 1983, a couple of other tool companies were selling products via catalog, but they mostly sold other companies' brands, so the product went through two or even three middlemen before it got to the consumer. That was this industry's business model in stores, too. A manufacturer such as Delta Machinery would sell products to a distributor, who would sell to dealers around the country, who would sell to consumers in individual stores. It was common to see Delta-branded machines in catalogs from various dealers at astronomical prices.

I came along and up-ended the industry. I sold my products directly to the end user at prices that were unheard-of. That model of selling is now called a "Direct to Consumer" sales model that merchants are gravitating towards. But you can have the best quality berries in the market, and they won't sell unless you scream loudly and let everyone know that you have incredible quality berries. It was essential that I get the word out, and magazine ads were the way to do it.

Magazine ads were expensive, costing anywhere from $1,000 to $10,000 per page, per issue, depending on circulation. The larger the circulation, the larger the potential buying audience, the more expensive the ad. The magazines were no dummies and knew the value of large circulations. A magazine like Popular Mechanics was cost-prohibitive for a start-up like me. I stayed within my means, focusing on magazines that charged $1,000 to $4,000 per full-page ad.

Existing ads from other companies were often little more than generic fluff, such as a picture of a bandsaw and a grandfather clock. Yes, I get it: you can make a grandfather clock with this bandsaw. I knew that customers wanted to know more about that bandsaw: capacity, motor size, dimensions, power requirements, and most important, cost! Remember, I was also a hobby user of my machines and viewed all marketing through the lens of a customer.

I created full-page ads that showed nine machines, neatly separated in boxes, each with specifications and price. The consumer could quickly go to his item of interest and find enough information to make a decision on the spot. Our ads also directed them to our phone number and catalog.

We were also creating a mailing list, adding customers who phoned in for any reason. Leili came into our warehouse office every morning after Shabir went to school, to enter names in the computer, pick up the mail, and take the previous day's sales to the bank before departing to return home, cook, pick up Shabir and take care of our homelife. I never had to worry about the home front and could concentrate on growing the business.

And that meant a catalog. The prevailing model for catalogs then was thin, cheap paper with a shelf life of about forty-five days. A customer would skim it, and if nothing caught his interest, discard it, knowing another would arrive in a few weeks.

I up-ended that model, too. I printed our catalog on thick, quality paper, with an even thicker, glossy card-stock cover. The cover was marked with the year, not week or month. I wanted to train our customers to keep the catalog and refer to it over the year.

At our warehouse office, Shirley, Leili, Gerry, and I, with our other office staff, would stuff catalogs into envelopes and toss them into U.S. Postal Service plastic tubs, then lug the tubs to the post office. Upon receipt of our catalog, customers would fill out the mail-order form in the back of the catalog and mail it in with a check or credit card number. Today, that seems like the age of Fred Flintstone, but it was both common and effective.

In the early days of Grizzly Imports, I prepared all the ads and wrote the catalog copy myself. (I had printed the first catalog in Taiwan but pivoted to local printing so I could keep better control.) I hired out photography to a local professional and got into my first battle, over copyright. He planned to keep copyright of the photos. I told him since I was paying for them, and if he wanted repeat business from me, the copyright needed to be mine. I wasn't going to be held hostage as to how and when I could use the photographs I paid for. I could do it myself, and I told him so. He agreed, and I got it in writing from him.

I created ads manually. I cut out a photo of the machine from the catalog, and I used the copy machine to shrink it to size. I pasted it in place, using a glue stick, and wrote copy around it. Then I would send that off, along with the professional's original photo, to a Seattle company that would put it into a format that magazines could accept. (My copier photo just showed them where to place the photographer's print.)

Today, when I use the cut-and-paste function on my laptop, I wonder if contemporary users know the term comes from when we cut with scissors and pasted with glue. Primitive? Yes. Effective? Very! The market heard my message and responded with a flurry of order forms and telephone calls to the warehouse office of Grizzly Imports. The bear was starting to roar.

Grizzly's Old Offices that we built in the "fishy" warehouse

Shirley & Staff stuffing catalogs to be mailed to customers

CHAPTER 23

Fresh Masala Chicken Curry or... Ugh!

L eili was sitting up in bed, propped against pillows, when I brought in the supper tray. "Oh, moong bean curry again, what a surprise!" Leili said, her smile fading as she lifted the cover off the plate. She was pregnant, and after previous miscarriages was on full bed rest, doctor's orders.

This meant I was doing the cooking. On Sundays, I'd prepare large quantities of a simple dish and freeze it in dinner-size portions for the week. My extensive menu selections were moong curry one week, and potato and eggplant curry the following week. This was the fourth evening this week we were having moong curry.

I pulled a chair up to her bedside and dug into my portion of the moong curry. It was Fall of 1984. I was working days at Grizzly in Bellingham, but we were living in Delta, a suburb of Vancouver, close to the U.S. border. Our U.S. immigration process had been underway for many months, and it would be many more before it would be final and we could move to Bellingham.

Meanwhile, we had to eat. I was famished. I scooped up the last of my moong curry and relaxed against my straight chair. I was so hungry every night that even eating my own repeat dish for a week tasted good once it was re-heated.

Leili had taken a couple of bites, but most of her portion remained untouched. I frowned. This wouldn't do. It is imperative that a pregnant woman be well nourished.

I mentioned the situation to a couple of my aunts living nearby. I told them (foolishly, it turned out) I could take care of myself, and it was only

Leili who needed decent meals. They promptly began sending over freshly prepared food for her every day. Fragrant masala chicken curry, rice pilau seasoned with cumin and cardamom, flavorful vegetable curries of every kind, biryani studded with nuts and dried fruits—at dinnertime, Leili now sat up straighter in bed, smiling as she lifted the cover off the plate, eyes closing with pleasure as she inhaled the scent of all the spices.

She devoured her meal every night. I gulped mine down, too, whether it was reheated moong curry or reheated eggplant and potato curry.

Every day, I commuted forty minutes from Delta to Bellingham, crossing the border at 6 a.m. and returning home about 6:30 p.m. Often I would go home for dinner and then take Leili and Shabir back with me to Bellingham (this was before she became pregnant) across the border again to work at Grizzly until 10 p.m, preparing orders, corresponding with overseas factories, and paying bills. In the early 1980s, crossing the border was easy, and the border agents got to know me. Border traffic back then was very light. Many mornings, if the agents weren't out in their booths yet, they'd look out the window from their office building and just wave me through from afar.

At Grizzly, shipping containers kept rolling in and the warehouse started filling up. I bought pallet racks, to make use of unused vertical air space to store smaller items. I added conveyors so small items that were picked and put in bins would roll down toward the packing tables. As orders flowed in, I hired more warehouse staff, more office staff, and bought new computer stations for the new staff. The IBM System/34 was upgraded to the new latest, fastest System/36. Customers flocked to the warehouse from all over Washington and Oregon, and I hired a terrific showroom salesman named Smitty (who remains with the company today, in its fourth decade). The place buzzed with excitement and energy; I had no time to think as it was constantly go, go, go!

In the midst of this, in 1985 our daughter Jamila was born in Vancouver General Hospital, a healthy 9 pound 8 ounce "tubster"--with, we would later find out, a discerning palate for the freshest, tastiest curries. I thanked my aunts, those excellent cooks, with gifts of beautiful 22 carat gold jewelry.

In 1986 when Jamila was just over a year old, our immigration into the U.S. finalized and our family of four moved to Bellingham. The entire immigration process had taken nearly three years.

I still needed to travel to Taiwan at least twice a year to develop new products and deal with quality assurance, but the fierce pace at the warehouse made it impossible to get away. I made the decision to close the business for the week of July 4, and the week between Christmas and New Year's, making it mandatory for employees to take vacation then too. This was the only way I could manage to travel out of the country. Often, I'd take Leili and the kids with me to Taiwan when I conducted business, adding a quick stopover in Hong Kong. I like to remember those days, holding Shabir by the hand and pushing Jamila in her stroller through the dirty, noisy alleys of Hong Kong. Little Jamila, about a year old then, would perk up in her stroller, eyes wide, taking in the sights, sounds, and smells of the vibrant city. Our visits overseas were quick as we'd return within the week.

Back in Bellingham, business kept booming. My ads and catalog were doing their work, and Grizzly was shipping product all over the country. But as orders increased, so did customer complaints. The complaints centered around the cost of shipping from Bellingham to the more densely populated East Coast, where the majority of our customers were, and the frequency of damage to our products while underway.

I discovered that when I shipped product from Bellingham, it would first go to the trucker's depot in Seattle, then transfer to another truck headed for a terminal in a metropolis somewhere en route, then get unloaded and reloaded onto another truck headed for the destination. Sometimes our crates were transferred five times before arriving.

Too much handling, by crews not known for their delicate touch, was causing damage to our machinery. Plus, shipping time was erratic, taking ten days to three weeks, since shipments sometimes sat for days at a depot as the trucking company waited for enough product to fill a truck.

The solution was to open a second location on the East Coast, and have product shipped there directly from Taiwan.

About the same time, a new office machine called a fax was coming on the market. A fax performed the same function as my Telex, but it could scan and send typed documents. I could take invoices and such, feed it into a fax, and simultaneously it would print on the other end, anywhere in the world. It could do this without rattling like a machine gun, as the Telex did. The advent of fax meant that if I were to open another branch in the eastern U.S., we could communicate instantly and accurately.

I ditched my new-looking Telex—it was not quite three years old, same as my company—and planned a fact-finding trip through the states of New York, New Jersey, and Pennsylvania, to look for a second home for Grizzly. I knew a perfect location wasn't possible, but I wanted to come as close to perfect as I could.

What I didn't know was that the perfect town was indeed out there, and they were ready and waiting for me.

CHAPTER 24

The Roar in the East

For Grizzly's new East Coast location, I'd narrowed the choices to potential cities in three states. In the spring of 1986, I flew east, rented a car, and drove to Syracuse and Binghamton in New York, Camden in New Jersey, and King of Prussia and Williamsport in Pennsylvania. I was looking for smaller towns with good highway connections that would allow customers to get to us easily and be a major thoroughfare for trucking routes.

My final stop was Williamsport, then a city of 32,000 in the northeast central part of the state. On my map, when I drew a 200-mile radius around Williamsport, I realized 40 million people lived in cities within that radius.

I liked Williamsport the moment I drove into town. Beautifully built churches showing the ornate construction of yesteryear stood on almost every block in the downtown. Steeples, stained glass, gothic arches, delicate stonework—I counted six churches within a few blocks. With so many churches for such a small town, the people here would be good, God-fearing, likely hardworking folk.

The city of Williamsport had built a spec "shell" warehouse to entice business to town. This Shell Building was 40,000 square feet, with 20-foot-high ceilings, just what I was looking for. This was a quality-built steel Shell Building consisting of a heavy-duty steel frame with steel walls and roof and a dirt floor, awaiting a buyer who could customize the finish to his requirements. Part of the appeal was that since the warehouse was already up, there would be no permitting issues or delays. Simple electrical and plumbing permits were all that would be required.

What I didn't know immediately was the history of the Shell Building. It seems that several years earlier, the city authorities had built an earlier version of a shell warehouse on this site, using a cheaper and lighter-duty steel construction, but it remained empty. As time passed with no buyer or tenant, the townsfolk's anger grew. One winter, a storm dumped 18 inches of snow on Williamsport overnight, followed by several more days of snow. The first shell warehouse collapsed.

The townsfolk's anger turned into fury. City funds had been spent, and the warehouse that had remained empty for years was now wrecked. But insurance covered it, and this time, a stronger building was constructed. Now the city fathers were under tremendous pressure from citizens to unload this white elephant quickly.

When I came rolling into town in April 1986, the new, quality Shell Building had just been completed. It looked attractive and was made more so by the terms that were offered to me. As in any small town, the guys at the Chamber were chummy with the bank manager who was chummy with the mayor who was chummy with the City Council members. They offered me the building for $550,000, and that included the six acres it sat on. They could arrange a low-interest loan at 1.5 percent through the Commonwealth of Pennsylvania, and the local bank would finance my down payment. Even the local contractor was part of this "boys club," and offered a good value on pouring the concrete floor and finishing the place to my requirements.

They were on me like fleas, and I sensed their desperation. I made an offer of $400,000. After a hastily convened City Council meeting the next afternoon, they accepted.

Work got underway almost immediately. All that was needed was floors, interior walls, electrical, heating, and offices. Construction was quickly completed, and in November and early December we started sending containers of product from Bellingham.

I hired local workers, who indeed turned out to be as hardworking as I'd imagined on that first day I drove into town. My Bellingham employees "biker" Gerry and Shirley, with a couple of others, transferred to Williamsport to get the new location up and running. Shirley was promoted to general manager, and Gerry to warehouse manager, of our new East Coast location. Training took place the last two weeks of December.

In January 1987 we held a grand opening of our new showroom and warehouse. The night before, twelve inches of snow had fallen, but we still had thirty brave souls who drove in for our opening.

As soon as it opened, growth accelerated vertically. It wasn't uncommon to see cars with plates from ten different states in the parking lot on a Saturday morning. Shipping costs with the local companies shrank to a fraction of the cost of shipping from the West Coast. Damages were way down, and customers were receiving product within a few days of ordering.

The East Coast bear was roaring!

PA Office Staff in Front of Shell Building

Shiraz with PA Staff in 1988

CHAPTER 25

Of Pearls and Jewels

Never had I seen so many jewelry stores in one place. The Kowloon area of Hong Kong, glittering with neon signs and buzzing with visitors from all over the world, offered all sorts of merchandise to the shoppers crowding its streets, including leather goods from rare hides such as kangaroo and crocodile; Lalique crystal; the latest cameras; and tailor shops that could sew a custom-made suit in a day. But it seemed as if every other shop on the street was a jewelry store.

My regular trips to Taiwan for Grizzly Imports sometimes included a day or two in Hong Kong. When I began to earn money in the mid-1980s, I started to buy jewelry for Leili there.

Even as a kid, I'd been fascinated by jewelry, especially diamonds and pearls. More recently I had read up on how to grade diamonds. Now in Kowloon, I used that knowledge to negotiate the best I could with the seasoned Chinese merchants. As I strolled the exotic streets, browsing shops and noting prices, an idea formed in my mind: why not start my own jewelry company and sell jewelry mail-order, as I was doing with machinery and tools?

Back in Bellingham, as Grizzly thrived, I started researching the jewelry business. I learned that the authentic cultured pearls I'd seen in Hong Kong came from the coast of Japan, where the pristine waters were perfect for cultured pearl farms. Pearl growers would pry open the oyster shell, carefully make an incision, and insert a tiny particle, like a grain of sand. The oyster would isolate the irritant and cover it in a substance called nacre. Over two to four years, the layers of nacre would form a pearl. The pearl would be delicately removed, and another particle inserted. Once harvested, pearls were sorted, graded, and sold through wholesale markets to exporters who would sell them to jewelers around the world. Pearls are measured in millimeters, rounded to the nearest 0.5 mm, and pearls larger than 7 mm that were perfectly round with high luster fetched the highest prices.

If I were going to sell pearl jewelry, I needed to know all about pearls and how to make jewelry with them. In 1987 I enrolled in a class on pearl grading and necklace-tying with the Gemological Institute of America. The initial studying and testing were done at home, via mail, then I traveled to GIA headquarters in California for three days of training and testing on-site.

When I walked in the classroom that first day, I realized I would be the only male in a class of thirty-two students.

We learned how to grade pearls by size, shape, color, luster, surface quality, and nacre quality. We learned different ways to tie a strand of pearls. Good pearl necklaces have a knot between each pearl so that if the string broke, only one pearl would fall loose while the rest of the necklace would still remain together. These knots had to be very tight against each pearl and required a special tool. One of the most complex pearl-tying methods was that of a V-shaped, multi-layered pearl necklace that required continuous knotting at an angle. Every pearl had a knot between it and the next one, and the knot had to be tight against the pearl. One mistake and it was all over; you'd have to cut your string and start over.

That particular V-shaped necklace-stringing served as our final test. We were allotted two hours to create the necklace. This is where I could shine! Years of working with my hands, of handling and combining metal parts that were often as small as a pearl, served me well. I focused on the materials before me and fell into a steady rhythm. I didn't look up, but every so often I'd hear a cry of anguish from a student who'd made a mistake.

After an hour and a half, I tied the last knot, well ahead of schedule, and ahead of all other students. The necklace lay before me, its six layers of lustrous 3mm beads smoothly connected in a perfect V shape.

Some of the students did not finish in time. Others had mishaps along the way. When the two hours were up, our instructor, an older woman, held up my necklace and said, "Shame on you, ladies. The only man here has finished before all of you."

Years of working with my hands had increased my dexterity.

With that behind me, it was time for a trip to Japan to buy pearls for my new company.

I swung open the heavy glass door, and Leili and I entered the reception lobby of a pearl-export business in Osaka, Japan. It was December 1987. The lobby was elegant, with marble floors, high ceilings, and deep, oversize leather sofas. We checked in with the receptionist, and shortly after a Japanese man about 6'2" came to meet us. He was the business owner and appeared to be in his early 60s. After a few minutes, I remarked on his height, unusual among Japanese.

"My father is British, my mother Japanese," he said. "I was born in Japan and have lived here all my life."

The pearls were kept on the third floor, and he ushered us into an elevator. As soon as we got in, Leili said to me in Gujarati, "Ah budho bo-waj handsome che," meaning "This old man is very handsome."

The owner turned to her with a broad smile and said, "Thank you."

I thought it was funny, but Leili was supremely embarrassed! The owner, who sold pearls to buyers from around the world, could speak about a dozen languages, and had many Indian Gujarati jewelers as his clients.

On the third floor, he unlocked a thick, metal safety door studded with rivets. The vault door swung open and he led us into a large, paneled room with lighting meant to simulate natural light. The room was lined with shelves that held hundreds of bowls, each filled with pearls sorted by size, grade, and color. He also had pearls that were in strings but not knotted into necklaces.

I had come to the right place! I ordered many different types of pearls, both stranded and loose.

I arranged payment via wire transfer and returned to Bellingham, and shortly after, the pearls arrived via air shipment. Now I put my training to use, using the specialized pearl-knotting tool with needle and thread, and knotted dozens of different types of pearl necklaces in preparation for the catalog of my new company, Elite Exclusives, Inc.

With the pearl jewelry underway, I now had to buy more and different jewelry for Elite Exclusives. I attended a jewelry show in Bangkok, made connections with sellers, and purchased bracelets, bangles, earrings, and necklaces made with 18 carat gold and diamonds, rubies, and sapphires. Once I had all the jewelry in hand, I had it and the pearls photographed, and launched my catalog. I advertised the products and the catalog in women's magazines.

We had fairly decent sales to start, but with time it grew evident that this type of product lent itself to stores where buyers could physically touch and try on jewelry before buying. Within a couple of years, it became clear that mail-order jewelry would not work. I stopped spending time on it and ceased operations.

Today, I think of my Elite Exclusives experience as "been there, done that." I have no regret that I tried it. If you don't try, you'll always wonder what might have been.

Win some, lose some. On to the next venture!

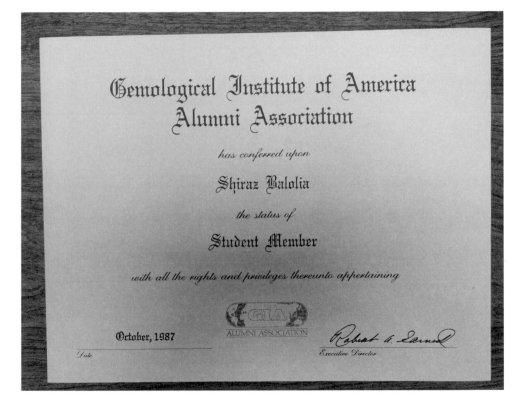

GIA Student Member Certificate

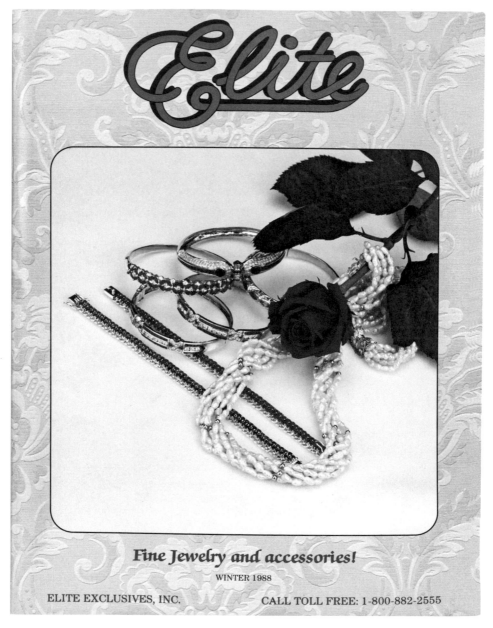

Elite Jewelry Catalog 1988

CHAPTER 26

More Space, More Companies

"Good morning, Grizzly Imports, how may I help you?" Linda, an order-taking employee at Grizzly, set aside her coffee cup, popped her phone headset on, and readied her pen over the order form pad as she answered the call.

"Hi, this is Ken calling from Missoula, I have your catalog in front of me, and I would like to order your G1021 planer and your G1022 table saw, plus the following accessories..." Ken continued with item after item as Linda scribbled madly onto the order form.

On the desk in front of her, two more phone lights blinked on. Next to Linda, two more order-takers at adjoining desks, wearing their phone headsets, punched the buttons on the phone system and greeted new customers, "Good morning, Grizzly Imports..."

Linda, still wearing her headset as she chatted with Ken the Customer, quickly added up the weight of Ken's items on a desk-top calculator. She swiveled in her chair to grab the big book of freight terminal codes, to look up the cost of shipping to Ken's zip code in Missoula.

By today's standards, order-taking at Grizzly Imports in the mid-1980s was primitive.

Since calculations were done manually, sometimes mistakes were made. If we overcharged the customer mistakenly, we would later send them a refund check for the difference, after we received the freight bills. If we undercharged, we ate it. An operator that made a lot of mistakes on billing, would often also make mistakes on the items ordered, and had to be either moved to a different position or terminated. The basis of running our business was to be accurate, and absolutely ethical and honest.

With no central order-taking program in our computer, order-takers took orders over the phone or via mail and filled out order forms in longhand. To figure the customer's shipping cost, they consulted printed reference books such as a large, bound atlas to look up the customer's location anywhere in the nation, and the big book of freight terminal codes. They passed the finished order forms to a specialized employee who entered the order in the IBM System/36, which printed the pick tickets that went to the warehouse for picking, packing, and shipping.

Opening our East Coast warehouse in January 1987 was like getting a booster shot in the arm. Sales just exploded! To keep the process simple for our order takers, we decided to use the Mississippi River as a dividing line. Any customer ordering by phone or mail from any state east of the Mississippi River would have it fulfilled by our Pennsylvania warehouse. Orders from any state west of the Mississippi would be fulfilled from Bellingham.

With the huge surge of business, we were running out of room at the Bellingham warehouse, for storage and office space. We maxed out the number of people we could squeeze into the offices, and warehouse space was even tighter. It got so bad that I actually throttled back on ads and promotions, to keep additional business from coming in. We talked our landlord Greg into renting us an additional 5,000 square feet. He moved the tall separating wall he had built a few years earlier and gave us the last available bay in the warehouse, bringing our total space to 20,000 square feet. It still wasn't enough.

I located a 10-acre parcel on Valencia Street in Bellingham and quickly drew plans for a 40,000-square-foot warehouse with plenty of office space and room to grow. It was sent to architects to draw up formally and apply for permits.

On Memorial Day 1989, we moved sixty shipping containers of product from our old, fish-smelling warehouse into the new Valencia Street location, which remains company headquarters today. We were able to build a proper temperature-controlled room for our System/36 with the proper computer wiring grids throughout the new office space.

Meanwhile, dealers across the nation had been inquiring for years if we would sell our products to them at a wholesale price. But since our business model was to sell directly to the end user at an already low price, there was no room for any further discount on bulk sales to dealers.

My solution was to start a new company, Woodstock International, Inc., specifically to serve dealers across the country at a wholesale-only price, and we did this in 1989 as soon as we moved into our new headquarters.

Woodstock started by selling smaller tools and dust-collection accessories and was immediately successful. So, here I was: selling to end-users via Grizzly, and selling to dealers via Woodstock--most of whom were Grizzly's competitors! It was a heavenly model for any businessperson.

From Grizzly, we knew what would sell well and what wouldn't at the retail level. We took products that had a higher profit margin and sold them to dealers through Woodstock at a discounted price. They were nicely packaged for retail display in dealers' stores and sold under several different brands trademarked by Woodstock. (Ultimately, Woodstock was so successful that it would make Inc. magazine's list of Top 500 companies in the USA in 1995 and 1996.)

That year, 1989, I also bought a company called Cascade Tools that sold millions of dollars annually of router bits and shaper cutters for the woodworking market. Router bits have various profiles such as what you would see on kitchen cabinets and doors and are used in portable routers. Shaper cutters also have profiles, are generally larger, and are used on stationary machines for cutting various profiles.

Cascade Tools was housed in the founder's home in Bellevue, a suburb of Seattle. He was storing all the product in his basement. He had hired neighborhood ladies to come in at various times to take orders, pack, and ship, a process that had grown cumbersome, time-consuming, and inefficient to be doing in a residential home.

By bringing Cascade Tools into our new warehouse, we were able to fine-tune the process, lowering shipping costs and delivery time to customers. We ran Cascade Tools as an independent company for several years before merging it into the mothership Grizzly.

That same year, 1989, my new hires included an 18-year-old warehouse man named Robert McCoy, a hardworking kid who worked his way over the years to management positions and ultimately became the President of Grizzly thirty years later.

We had the space, we had the people, we had the infrastructure. Our increasing success brought with it stronger financial resources. The bank loved our success, offering us a decent-sized line of credit to borrow money for growth. We could expand and branch into other businesses. My imagination was free to run wild. The floodgates had opened.

18 Yr Old Robert McCoy, Warehouse Employee would go on to become the President of Grizzly 30 Years later.

CHAPTER 27

The Pilots, the Billionaire, and the Feds

The candlelight flickered over the pressed linen tablecloth and the sound system played soft jazz as our host began to tell a story. On this rainy Pacific Northwest evening in 1989, Leili and I were dinner guests of Chris and Gail Bach at an Italian restaurant in Bellingham. We had met them a few months before.

"A bunch of TWA pilots are sitting around an airport lounge in Singapore," Chris says. "It's the spring of 1970. They're talking about their love of flying, and their conversation takes on a serious tone, since some of these guys are nearing retirement. One of the older guys says, 'Wouldn't it be great if we could buy a little island somewhere, build a runway on it, and fly our small planes right to our new waterfront retirement homes?'"

Chris pauses and sips red wine. Outside the restaurant, rain batters against the window. Leili leans closer to hear.

"These pilots love the idea," Chris says, warming to his story. "They have the dough. Some have connections with the Federal Aviation Administration to get permitting for a runway. Fourteen of them commit to the plan. They locate and buy a wild island off the coast of Washington state, and subdivide it into multiple five and ten-acre parcels, all owned by the pilots."

"What island?" I ask. We were quite familiar with the San Juan archipelago, a wonderland of numerous islands, big and small, off the coast of Washington near Bellingham and Seattle.

"Allan Island," Chris says. "You might not know that one. It's 290 acres, sort of southwest of the city of Anacortes, just south of us. It's not too far from the U.S. Naval Air Station on Whidbey Island. Anyway, the pilots put in a 3,000-foot grass runway on Allan Island, big enough to land Lear jets on."

Chris takes another sip of red wine, pauses.

"What happened?" I ask. "Did they live happily ever after?"

"Not exactly." Chris sets down his glass. "That runway was expensive. A marina is built, as well as a nice log home near the beach at the marina, but as years go by, some of the pilots get divorced, some die of old age, some run out of money. Their grand idea fades away. Twenty years have passed since they walked into that airport lounge in Singapore, which brings us to today, 1989."

Chris looks at me, then at Leili. "About 80 percent of current owners on Allan Island want to sell. There's profit to be made if those properties can be sold to wealthy city folks with planes who want an island getaway. Gail and I want to ask if you're interested in being investment partners with us on this project."

We'd first met Chris and Gail Bach earlier that year, on a sunny summer day when we'd driven from our Bellingham home twenty miles north to the small town of Birch Bay, in the far northwest corner of Washington state near the Canadian border. Leili had seen an ad for homebuilding lots on the Birch Bay golf course and wanted to take a look.

As we turned into the gated development, we saw lush green grass on neat, attractive lots abutting a beautiful golf course lined with majestic Pacific Northwest firs and cedars. On the course, golfers in colorful attire swung clubs and hopped into bright white carts. Chris and Gail, who were in charge of the development and selling the lots, greeted us and showed us around.

Leili and I knew that Birch Bay attracted Canadian buyers from Greater Vancouver. Compared to prices there, the Birch Bay lots at $20,000 to $24,000 each were a screaming deal.

We liked what we saw, negotiated a bulk price of $20,000 each for three lots, and soon closed the deal.

A month later, Gail Bach phoned and asked if I wanted to sell. Sell?! We'd just bought them! I was doubly surprised since there had been other lots available for sale when we purchased.

Gail said they'd placed an ad in the Vancouver Sun and within a week had sold every remaining lot to Canadians, each at full asking price. Gail said we'd gotten a good deal on our three lots, and if we wanted to sell them, we could likely make 20 percent profit after their commission. Since Gail and Chris had a waiting list of buyers, we could sell quickly.

We said yes. Within a week, we'd sold all three lots for a tidy profit on an extremely short-term investment. Our first taste of the real estate business was delicious!

A few months later, when Chris and Gail invited us to dinner on that rainy evening at the Italian restaurant, we thought they meant to celebrate our quick sale, but they had something bigger in mind—Allan Island. The Bachs had completed their work in Birch Bay and identified the island as their next real estate project.

We were interested, but I said the island would be worth more if we could own the whole island. They replied they'd already approached everyone.

"Go back and speak to every owner separately," I said. "That could work. If you can secure 100 percent of the lots, I'm in."

Chris and Gail were both good salespeople and negotiators, and this time secured all current owners at reasonable prices except for two holdouts, who wouldn't budge. I told them to "throw money" at the two holdouts, and we could average the cost per acre of the whole island. We wound up paying almost double to each holdout, but we secured the entire island for a total of $3.14 million. We also negotiated owner financing, which meant we paid a small down payment and the owners would carry the balance at a very low interest rate for five years.

Our overall cash outlay for the island was less than $500,000. We formed a 50-50 partnership, Balolia Bach Properties. We agreed that for the first year, I could make decisions without their agreement, otherwise a 50-50 partnership could stall. The second year, the Bachs could make decisions without my agreement. They would live in the log home on the island, do maintenance around the island, and help with marketing and promotion.

We discussed an asking price for the island. Without thinking about it too much, I said $16 million.

"What?!" exclaimed Chris. "Where did you come up with that price?"

Chris, whose business was real estate, started to educate me on how real estate prices are set, saying it required studying "comps," meaning sale prices of similar properties. Recent comps are generally an indication of what the property would sell for.

"Chris," I said. "How many pristine 290-acre islands are for sale on the west coast, or for that matter anywhere in the country? How many have a runway for a Lear jet?"

The value of this island was in its existing runway. In current times, it would be impossible to get such a thing permitted. I told him we'd market Allan Island to billionaires such as Bill Gates, Paul Allen, the Sultan of Brunei, Donald Trump, the Sam Walton family, the owners of Oakley sunglasses, and others all over the world who could fly in to their private getaway in their own planes.

"There is something magical about owning an island," I said. "Billionaires won't be able to resist this beauty."

The Bachs initially argued against the $16 million price but ultimately deferred since I was the managing partner for that year.

We created a beautiful brochure and mailed it to super-rich people around the world, and a Japanese hotel group bit. They wanted to build an exclusive resort. We agreed to sell the island for $13.5 million; they even paid us $320,000 in nonrefundable earnest money.

On the morning the sale was to close, Chris got a call from their attorney. They would not be buying the island, due to an internal conflict over its management.

The buyer backing out at literally the last minute had a harsher impact on Chris than on me. I am practical and only believe a sale when the cash is in my hands. Oh well, at least we had their non-refundable $320K!

We were now into our second year, and Chris and Gail became the managing partners with the last word on decisions. They wanted to price the island for a quick sale at $5 million, but I was able to nudge it higher, pointing out we'd almost sold it for $13.5. They priced it at $8.5 million.

In flew Paul Allen, known for co-founding Microsoft Corporation, and we sold Allan Island to him for just under $7 million. Allen unleashed his attorneys and architects on us and completed the purchase a few months later under the name of a trust. We signed a confidentiality agreement that prevented us from telling anyone who the buyer was.

Counting the nonrefundable $320,000 we'd gotten from the Japanese hotel group, our $7 million-plus sale was not bad for an initial cash outlay of $500,000.

But the story didn't end there. Three months after we sold, I was deep into paperwork at my desk at Grizzly when a tall, imposing man strode into our offices upstairs, walking right past our receptionist, and barged into my office holding up a badge.

I looked up thinking, *Who the hell is this guy?*

"Shiraz Balolia?" he barked the question. Startled, I nodded.

"I'm with the DEA, Drug Enforcement Agency." Without invitation, he plunked down in my visitor chair and crossed his legs. "You recently sold an island," he stated as a matter of fact. He leaned forward, his eyes boring into mine. "To whom did you sell it?"

"We signed a confidentiality agreement," I said.

He didn't speak, just continued glaring at me.

"But," I went on, prudently, "since you're with the federal government and can find out this type of information anyway, I'll tell you. Paul Allen."

"Thank you," he said, stood up, thought for a second, and walked out.

It turned out that several federal agencies were keeping an eye on little Allan Island, near the Naval Air Station on Whidbey Island. Beautiful Allan Island, with its marina and airstrip, would have been perfect for drug smugglers and other nefarious characters.

With the island sold, Gail and Chris Bach moved on to other projects farther afield. As for me, I'd enjoyed my initial taste of the real estate market so much that in 1991, I launched a company named Elite Developments, Inc., to continue buying and selling real estate in the Bellingham area.

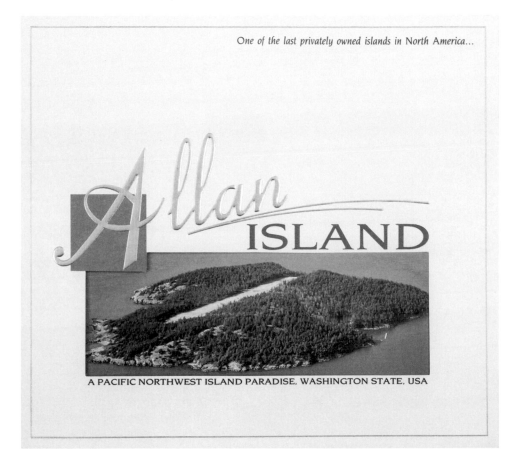

One of the last privately owned islands in North America...

A PACIFIC NORTHWEST ISLAND PARADISE, WASHINGTON STATE, USA

Allan Island

A Bad Case of Capitalism

CHAPTER 28

Here Comes China

Life at Grizzly had two speeds: fast and faster. By the early 1990s, I had put management in place at headquarters in Bellingham and was making two trips to our Pennsylvania location and two trips to Taiwan every year.

We were hiring more people, increasing our variety of products, and stocking more inventory at both locations. Woodstock International, the company I'd started in 1989 that sold only to dealers, was likewise growing quickly as we sold to more and more dealers across the country. We were now carrying a lot of smaller tools to supplement the large machines.

One popular small item was the Forstner bit, a specialized bit that drills smooth holes with flat bottoms. Invented by American Benjamin Forstner in 1874, it had been recently developed further by Austrian makers.

Austrian-made Forstner bits had a reputation for quality. These bits came in sizes from ¼ inch to 2 inches diameter and were often sold in 16-piece sets. Taiwanese manufacturers quickly copied the Austrian bits and came out with an identical set for less than half the cost. Grizzly sold both Austrian and Taiwanese sets, to give our customers a choice in perceived quality.

One day out of the blue, I got a call from a Mr. Mortimer Schwartz of Dollar Trading Company. Mr. Schwartz was a New York businessman who claimed he'd developed Forstner bits in China that were as good or better than the Austrian ones on the market.

Sitting at my desk in my second-floor office at the warehouse in Bellingham, I raised my eyebrows. *Sure you did*, I thought. *That's just a sales pitch*.

But I said only, "Oh? Tell me, how are they better?"

"I could tell you," Mr. Schwartz rasped in his New York accent into the phone, "but you wouldn't believe me. I'm going to send you a set so you can try them yourself."

When the Chinese-made Forstner bit set arrived in the mail, I sent it downstairs to Grizzly's quality control department, asking the supervisor to test it against the Austrian-made set that we carried. A few hours later, the supervisor climbed the stairs and knocked on my office door.

"Boss, I have to tell you, those Chinese Forstner bits are sharper, and they drill cleaner holes than the Austrian ones," he said.

"Really?" I replied. "You did identical tests, using the same-size bits, same wood?"

The supervisor nodded. "I didn't believe it either, so we tested it a few times with several different sizes."

I wanted to see this. I went downstairs and was able to confirm his report by drilling the holes in hardwood myself. Frankly, I was equally surprised as these Chinese-made sets were 30 percent cheaper than the Taiwanese ones, which were already about half the cost of the Austrian ones.

We negotiated a very good price with Mr. Schwartz for large quantities of those sets, promoted them at a good price in all the magazines—and sold them by the thousands. Sayonara Austria!

My policy as a businessman has always been to pay my bills on time, in most cases ahead of time. I personally ingrained this into my employees in the accounting department. Usually we'd get a discount of 1 percent for paying within ten days of receipt of goods, and we almost always took this discount by paying as soon as we received the invoice. These little 1 percent discounts added up to thousands of dollars each year.

During these years, I was still signing all the checks at Grizzly, so every week I'd see invoices ranging from $5,000 to $30,000 from Dollar Trading Company. Besides their Forstner bit sets, we also started buying other small tools from them, such as chisels, drill bits, sharpening stones, and other accessories for the woodworking industry. One day, I was signing a particularly large check to Dollar Trading, when I thought, *Why don't I just buy this company?*

I picked up the phone, called the number on the invoice, and got Mr. Schwartz on the line. After greetings, I got to the point.

"Do you want to sell your company?" I asked.

Mr. Schwartz was a savvy businessman and polished negotiator. Without missing a beat, he answered no, he wasn't thinking of selling.

"If you ever do want to sell your company, I'd be interested," I said.

We carried on chatting, and I asked about his family. He told me he was in his late 60s, with a daughter and grandchildren on the West Coast.

A week later, Mr. Schwartz called me and said though he wasn't ready to sell, he did want to spend more time with those grandkids out west, and he might be convinced if the price were right…

The hook was on! We discussed his overall sales, and costs of products. He was open with information about costs, and how many units he sold and to whom. We came to an agreement on the phone for a price range for his business, pending a visit from him to my office for further discussion.

When he visited Grizzly in Bellingham, we were both impressed with each other personally as well as business-wise. He was satisfied that I would do a good job with his company, and I knew the complex relationships he had built up in China would become mine along with the company. Plus, I would gain his customer list of active dealers he was selling to, and promptly offer them the full variety of Woodstock's products. Oooh--I was loving this!

I purchased Dollar Trading in 1993 and instantly acquired all the contacts with the various state-owned and small factories that Mr. Schwartz had painstakingly developed over years in China. In the early 1990s and before, it was extremely difficult to do business in China, with government red tape, few flights, and no highways or modern transportation within the country. Mr. Schwartz was one of the very few Americans who ventured to China, traveling in dirty and overcrowded buses, staying in lodging where cockroaches commonly scurried across the floor, and sipping tea from stained and cracked teacups that sometimes imparted more than tea.

His strongest connection was with the China Eastern Company, a government-owned exporter that controlled smaller factories that manufactured and exported a variety of products, and his main contact there was an engineer named Cindy Zhang. I began communicating with Cindy and worked with her to add many other small items made in China at very good prices.

Thus began our foray into doing business in China, by instantly getting all the contacts Mr. Schwartz had developed at great discomfort and peril.

CHAPTER 29

"While You're Reading This, He's Starting Another Company"

The success of my newest acquisition, Dollar Trading Company, opened my eyes to new possibilities. Where else might opportunity lie?

I kept watch on the checks I was signing to our vendors for products we had bought and received, and how well these items would fit with Woodstock's offerings to its dealers.

A company named Magna-Set caught my eye. A Magna-set is a device that precisely adjusts the knives on the cutterheads of woodworking planers and jointers. It got its name because it involved specialized magnets in its jigs. (A jig is a custom-made fixture that is used for holding and locating parts in place for repeatability.) Magna-Set manufactured everything in the United States, which was a plus for me. I bought all the dies and specialized manufacturing equipment and brought all Magna-set manufacturing in-house to our Grizzly warehouse in Bellingham, which created a few extra jobs as well. I later changed the names of the Magna-set jigs to Jointer Pal and Planer Pal. We have sold thousands of those jigs over the years.

A company named Pro-Stik captured my attention next. A Pro-Stik is a bar of crepe-like, light-colored rubber, 2 by 2 by 12 inches. It's used for removing the sticky sawdust that builds up on sanding belts and discs. The user holds a Pro-Stik against the moving belt or disc to clean it, restoring the belt or disc to near-new condition.

Pro-Stik was a small, single-product company, but an important one because we sold thousands of belts and discs to customers, and the only place these rubber products were produced was in war-torn Sri Lanka. Sri Lanka's civil war had erupted in 1983 and would last twenty-six years, eventually killing more than 100,000 civilians. I sure as hell was not going to Sri Lanka to source a supplier!

The owner of Pro-Stik, in his 40s at that point, had traveled to Sri Lanka to develop this product, likely dodging bullets from Tamil Tiger rebels in the process. He sold his belt-and-disc-cleaning rubber bars to dealers of woodworking machinery and sanding belts and discs in the United States. He was tired of running the company and ready to sell. When I called him, I got the feeling that he was not making ends meet with just a one-item company. But it would fit in great with Woodstock, and I would have no additional costs of management such as accounting, sales, overseas ordering, or marketing. All that would get folded into our existing departments. I immediately merged this acquisition and its dealers into Woodstock. During these years I was running Woodstock concurrently with Grizzly out of our Bellingham and Williamsport, Pennsylvania warehouses.

The world seemed wide open with possibilities! I was looking to do business in my personal areas of interest, one of which was art. It could be interesting to import sculptures from Italy and sell them via catalog in the United States. By this time, Grizzly had a great little graphics/art department; we did all design and artwork in-house for our catalogs, ads, and other printed material. Since we were already set up and running, marketing was easy for us. Why not make use of what we already had?

In 1993 I started a company, naming it Sculptures of Venice, Inc., to import marble sculptures, lamps, coffee tables, and other items from Italy. I found a boutique, family-owned manufacturer of marble sculptures in the Sicily region and negotiated a two-year price guarantee as well as an exclusive sales agreement for the United States. The first container of products came in, we photographed the items, and produced a catalog. We rented mailing lists of subscribers to architectural magazines, and other professionals, and mailed out our catalogs. As soon as our catalog landed in the hands of potential customers, orders rolled in—and that is when the problems began.

Marble items are extremely susceptible to damage in shipping, and we had a huge number of claims. While the manufacturer had beautiful things carved by talented artists, they had no understanding of business etiquette. When I tried to place a second order, they raised prices almost 50 percent even though we had a written agreement about price guarantees for two years.

I did not want to deal with an unsophisticated vendor who could not be trusted. I wasn't about to hold their feet to the fire on the price guarantee agreement they had signed, either. Remember, Sicily was Mafia headquarters and I had no intention of seeing the shine of a stiletto blade in the dark of the night! With the increase in damage issues, I chose to abandon this venture and wrapped up Sculptures of Venice.

Besides art, I'd always been interested in knives and swords. As a teen in Africa, I'd carried a switchblade in my pocket, though luckily I never had to use it to defend myself. In 1994 I started a company called Grizzly Knife & Tackle, Inc., and began selling knives and cutlery of well-known brands such as Gutmann Cutlery, Buck, and Gerber. I also designed my own brand of knives, producing it under the name Junglee. In Gujarati, junglee means a wild man of the jungle, similar to Tarzan.

I received numerous patents for knife design, creating special handles and blade shapes of knives and swords that did not exist on the market. These patents allowed our line of Junglee knives to have unique shapes and handles that no other knife company could duplicate. I had them manufactured in Japan and Taiwan under the Junglee brand. I made a couple of trips to Seki, Japan, a small town famous for its sword and knife makers. My Junglee brand became prominent in the knife industry.

Grizzly Knife & Tackle was already selling knives made by Gutmann Cutlery, a famous company founded in 1947, when the opportunity to buy it arose. Guttmann produced knives of very high quality, mostly in Germany and Japan. I bought this company in 1994 and merged it into Grizzly Knife & Tackle. Now we were selling cutlery both ways: retail directly to consumers, and wholesale to major dealers and catalogs throughout the United States.

All this business activity caught the attention of the media. In 1996, Inc. magazine did an article on me headlined "While You're Reading This, He's Starting Another Business," with the sub-headline "An entrepreneur who currently runs 11 companies explains why he has such a bad case of capitalism." The article opened with this paragraph:

"I see opportunities out there that are so easy, I can't help myself," says Shiraz Balolia. Maybe that's why Balolia runs eleven companies in addition to Woodstock International, a wholesale distributor of woodworking tools. The Kenyan-born entrepreneur's enterprises range from cutlery to jewelry to sculpture to real estate development. To gain an edge on his fellow cutlery retailers, Balolia started Grizzly Knife & Tackle, a wholesaler—which supplies products to retailers. He hopes Grizzly will be able to count "almost every single one of our competitors" as a customer.

"I have a bad case of capitalism," he says.

(Over the coming decades, I would eventually own twenty-nine companies—just not all at the same time.)

Meanwhile, the mothership Grizzly continued to grow, as did Woodstock. I was always looking for the Next Big Thing, and I kept seeing Bass Pro Shops and Cabela's do an incredible volume of business in outdoor recreation products through their showrooms and catalogs. Always, when we were dealing with vendors, those two names came up. Plus, I was experiencing success in the knife industry. All this led me in 1994 to launch another company, Gorilla and Sons, Inc. to sell fishing, camping, and hunting gear.

It would be my first big mistake. I was about to lose millions.

Some of the Catalogs of Various Businesses I Started/Owned.

A Bad Case of Capitalism

CHAPTER 30

The Big Fail

To understand why I started the outdoor-recreation gear company Gorilla and Sons, you have to remember that I spent my early childhood in Mombasa, Kenya. Mombasa is an island connected to the African mainland by a causeway. Growing up, I loved the water and I loved fishing.

With no money, and not knowing what modern fishing poles looked like, most of us kids on the docks in Mombasa used a bamboo stick about five feet long with a screw eye on one end, through which we would run a fishing line. We'd tie a hook on the line, keeping the balance of line on a small spool. We'd lower the baited hook into the water and wait for a fish to bite. If we wanted to cast the line out further, we had to grab the line by hand and throw it out. Primitive, but effective. We fished year-round, no fishing licenses needed, and usually caught two to four in an afternoon. The saltwater fish were a local species that looked like trout, about eight to ten inches long and very delicious. I brought them home, deep fried them crispy brown, added salt and lemon juice, and gulped them down before anyone else in the home could ask for a taste. Mmm, mmm good!

At age nineteen when I moved to Vancouver, Canada, I was amazed by the quality and variety of fishing rods. Fishing for salmon meant using a long, flexible rod. Fishing for halibut required a shorter, thicker rod.

Living in the Pacific Northwest (in Vancouver or in Bellingham, where we moved in 1986) my enjoyment of fishing deepened. A king salmon, also known as a chinook, will make several runs before being landed. A silver salmon, known as a coho, will put up a furious but short-lived fight.

A halibut will make you feel as if you're hauling up a barn door from the ocean floor. Then, when you get it near the boat, it will look at you as if to say, "Oh, I'm hooked, see ya!" and dive back down to the bottom. By the time you land a decent-size halibut, your arms will feel like Jell-O.

I realized I'd always lived by the water: Mombasa, Vancouver, San Diego, Bellingham. When I started Grizzly Knife & Tackle in 1994, our first main products were fishing reels imported from South Korea. These were high quality reels that we sold wholesale to dealers. At trade shows, we displayed these along with fly tying vises that we imported from India. We took orders at the shows and shipped product later. At these trade shows, I'd watch the buzz around Cabela's and Bass Pro Shops; at home, I received their catalogs showing their fishing, hunting, and outdoor products. While most of their products were known brand names, I noticed they were also selling items they imported themselves from Taiwan.

I was already experienced in doing business in Taiwan. This would be a good opportunity to get into a new business, using our existing infrastructure, people, and distribution.

I needed a catchy name for my new venture and decided on Gorilla and Sons. I asked our in-house artist, Ray Goto, to come up with a cartoon logo of a gorilla that looked like a range warden. In a matter of minutes, our gifted artist came up with the perfect logo: a gorilla in a safari hat with his arms crossed.

Gorilla and Sons needed plenty of product lines to catch the customer's interest. In these pre-internet days, we had to create a catalog, place ads in major outdoor magazines, and send out multiple press releases for multiple products. We met with suppliers of big brands of outdoor recreational equipment—brands with stringent selling structures that reminded me of my early days in the machinery business, where the major players had their distribution channels set and didn't want any upstarts. But our Grizzly offices in Bellingham were attractive, and when the salespeople of big companies came to visit, they could see we had the ability to place big orders. We got good pricing but had to commit to large orders to do so.

We ordered different types of fishing line, all kinds of rods including expensive ones by G. Loomis, reels, hooks, tackle boxes and more, much of which I hadn't known existed. And that was just one category. We still needed to address clothing, camping, and hunting gear, though we did not sell guns.

The outdoor clothing business was complicated. Camouflage clothing could be purchased only from certain licensed suppliers. All clothing had to be preordered in January for delivery in late summer for the Fall season, which meant we had to guess as to sizes, colors, and amounts to order. Since we didn't yet have experience in what clothing would sell, ordering in January felt like a shot in the dark.

Once the selling season was underway, if you sold out of an item, you couldn't just call up and ask for more. There was no more. Apparel manufacturers made only what had been preordered back in January.

The outdoor shoe business was similar. In our first season of Gorilla and Sons, a certain boot sold really well, and we sold out of our full order of thirty pairs within two weeks. When we called to order more, they told us that design had been discontinued. The new footwear wouldn't be shown until the next SHOT show (the Shooting, Hunting, Outdoor Trade show) in January, and we could choose the latest designs and order then.

The first year, 1994, was a total mess. We had preordered more than

$1 million worth of products. Each item had to be photographed and have catalog copy written for it, and ads placed in magazines. When all this product arrived, we didn't have enough space in the warehouse to organize it properly. We had to put product wherever we could. New employees had been hired, current employees were working overtime, and managers were logging long hours, all of which impacted our mothership of Grizzly. Effort that would have gone toward growth and marketing for Grizzly's products was instead channeled toward Gorilla and Sons.

Once the catalog landed in customers' homes, a lot of the products sold well. But not having stocked products appropriately in the warehouse made picking, packing, and shipping inefficient. To make things worse, many products, especially shoes and clothing, did not sell well. What we didn't sell, we were stuck with. What we did sell well could not be reordered due to the nature of the industry. Discounting remaining products was cumbersome and didn't result in the sales volume necessary to unload the leftover clothing, even at a loss.

Right after we mailed out the catalog, it was time to reorder for the next season--before having any track record of what was going to sell well. It was like a dog chasing its tail! I began to see that in this industry, you'd need at least half a dozen years' experience in selling different types of apparel to learn how to successfully manage it. Even so, you often see established companies offering heavily discounted clothing and footwear at the end of a season.

Our best solution to selling leftover product was to open a retail store. Bellingham is a strong market for outdoor gear, and with a local store, we could service it easily. We signed a three-year lease on a space in downtown Bellingham and put a huge amount of effort into its launch. Though we had hired more employees, we had to depend on Grizzly's current managerial staff. Once more, Grizzly was being robbed of their time and effort as they tended to Gorilla and Sons.

Even with all that, it became clear that a retail store needed yet more nurturing. And it wasn't fulfilling its purpose: we were not able to sell all our leftover merchandise in that store. After launching and running Gorilla and Sons for just over two years, we had lost more than $3 million, counting wages, rent, catalogs, unsold product, and unprofitable product. (That included $1 million worth of leftover outdoor product that we eventually donated to clubs and charities.) Plus, the effort that was being siphoned away from Grizzly Imports toward Gorilla and Sons was hampering the growth of our mothership machinery business.

Barely eighteen months after opening the retail store, I made the hard decision in 1996 to shut down Gorilla and Sons entirely, take the losses, and consider it a lesson learned. We even paid off the balance of the lease on the retail store. My only solace was that we were strong enough financially to withstand the loss.

As boxers say, "If you have a glass jaw, don't enter the boxing ring, because sooner or later someone's going to land a hard punch on your jaw."

Gorilla and Sons delivered a heavy punch to my jaw. Luckily, it wasn't made of glass.

Gorilla & Sons Closing Down Billboard

CHAPTER 31

Becoming American

During those go-go-go years of the early 1990s, in the midst of launching company after company, I paused for a proud day in October 1993, when Leili and I with our two children traveled to Seattle for the naturalization ceremony that would make us full American citizens.

When I was growing up in Africa, anything American caught my interest. Bazooka Joe chewing gum, with its comic strip wrapped inside, entertained me. Comic books such as Superman or Batman, with ads in the back enticing young readers to send in for miscellaneous gadgets and then sell them at a profit, fascinated me. Wow—American kids could buy and sell items to earn pocket money?

Later, as an 18-year-old working as a costing clerk at a hardware store in Nairobi, on payday I would walk across the street to a coin shop. My favorite coins to buy were Morgan silver dollars from the 1870s and '80s. The physical size of the coins impressed me, and they felt nice and weighty in my hand. The big eagle with the words "In God We Trust" made me feel that America was a proud and honorable country.

Working at Apollo Dry Cleaners in Nairobi, I chatted with many expatriate customers, but the British and American customers stood out. At that time, about 1970, I felt the British had more of a colonial attitude. Maybe it was Headmaster Cockry's beatings that colored my opinion, but Kenya was a former British colony, and some British customers still talked down to many of us in society. The American customers were friendlier, easygoing, and fun to talk to.

One American woman in particular loved to talk when she came in.

When she dropped off her fine clothing, we often chatted about popular music. She loved the country singer-songwriters Jim Reeves and Del Reeves (oddly, they are not related). Since I often listened to American music on my record player, I bought a few of their LP albums, those large vinyl records sought by collectors today.

Of course, like so many youthful collectors, when I left Africa, I sold my large and varied collection of LPs for the pittance of just 230 shillings (about $13 then). Now I wish I had that vintage vinyl back!

Later on, I also corrected my previous opinions of the Brits, after getting to know my brother Akbar's wife Pat, and wonderful British shooting friends. But in any case, as a child and teen in Kenya, one of my goals was to become an American and live in the United States.

As an immigrant from a third-world country, the USA was the ultimate destination, the promised land of freedom to say and do anything, a place offering boundless opportunity. In Kenya in 1970, if one were to loudly say something derogatory about then-President Jomo Kenyatta, that speaker would most likely disappear, never to be heard from again. In many countries today, the government can limit your movement; there is no such thing as unemployment insurance. If you lose your job, you are on your own, as there is no government assistance when you are in need. Safe, clean water is scarce and open sewers take the place of sidewalks. In the 1970s in certain Asian countries, if the family breadwinner spoke out against the political climate and disappeared, his family would suffer.

As someone born in a third-world country, who now conducts business in several countries and has traveled the world visiting about thirty different countries, I have a perspective that some people born here in the USA may lack. It shocks and upsets me to see some Americans show disrespect to their country, a country that offers them a level of health, safety, and opportunity unheard-of in many other places. Simply put, they don't know what they have, and to blame the government for their problems is illogical. Burning or stomping on our flag just shows ignorance.

I can personally attest that this is the best country to live in. Most immigrants will agree with me. Anything is possible here. You are limited only by your imagination and ambition. As a proud American who came from another country, I can say from my heart: do not take this amazing country for granted. It is truly the land of freedom and boundless opportunity.

It had long been my dream to become an American myself, and after five years of being green card holders and residing continuously in the United States, in October 1993 Leili and I with our children walked into a wonderful oak-paneled room with high ceilings in Seattle, raised our hands in front of a judge, and pledged allegiance to the United States of America.

Woohoo--we were now Americans!

CHAPTER 32

Taiwan Attacks!

T aiwan in the early days was like the Wild West: normal rules of conversation didn't necessarily apply. In the 1980s and 1990s, what was said to your face in a meeting might not be what was actually meant.

One problem with factories in Taiwan was that they would sell to anyone who came along, just changing colors and labels on the products. This was more prevalent in the early days when I started in business. An example was the factory to which I'd sent a sample machine a couple of years earlier through six-girlfriend James, my Taiwanese friend and agent (the one who'd come to a business dinner the first day I met him with three girlfriends on each arm). This factory was now making a particular machine for us exclusively. On a subsequent trip to Taiwan in 1984, I decided to pay this factory a surprise visit.

The factory's small front office had cracked walls featuring a calendar stuck up with tape. James and I entered and saw the factory boss, Chang, seated in a wooden chair with broken arms, behind an old metal desk covered with teetering stacks of paper and greasy, fingerprint-smudged files. When he saw it was us, Chang leapt up with a look of alarm. Instant red flag! As James and Chang began talking in their local Taiwanese dialect, I walked through a side door in the office directly into the factory to see what they were working on—and saw that the product Chang was making for us, supposedly on an exclusive basis, was being manufactured with a different brand on it.

This called for an extreme response, and it had to be visual since Chang spoke no English. I shouted and raised my arms in obvious anger.

Chang responded by sprinting around the factory, ripping the pirate-brand plates off the machines, all the while shouting at his workers as if it were their fault. He told James that it was a mistake and the workers had put the labels on the wrong machines. The problem was that there were no other machines on the floor.

I spent the next two hours in Chang's office, writing out a contract on a writing pad atop my briefcase balanced on my lap. Up until now the agreement had been verbal. This time the contract about exclusivity would not be misunderstood. James translated it for Chang. Chang assured us he understood it, but as he bent over the document to sign, I noticed a sly look on his face.

I signed the contract as well, and we made copies for each of us.

Next day, James and I were out and about visiting factories when I decided to go back to Chang's factory for another surprise drop-in. This time we walked directly into the factory and saw the workers once more installing fresh pirate-brand name plates on the products from which Chang had ripped off labels the previous day.

"Where is Chang?" I demanded of the nearest factory worker.

A flurry of talk ensued as James translated, then turned to me. "Chang is at his friend's factory next door."

I told James to ask one of the workers to go get Chang.

Around us, factory workers paused at their tasks, obviously enjoying the unfolding drama. James had barely finished translating when the nearest factory worker abandoned his station and ran out the door, presumably to fetch Chang. I stalked off the factory floor into the little front office, James at my side. Neither of us bothered to take a seat in the rickety straight-backed wood chairs meant for guests.

We didn't have to wait long. Chang appeared moments later, his face flushed with sweat, speaking rapidly to James. But his excuses, and James's translation, snapped off mid-sentence as I opened my briefcase, took out our contract, tore it to pieces, and threw it all down on his nicked-rosewood

186

coffee table.

I looked Chang in the eye as I swept up a fistful of the torn contract pieces off the coffee table, made some obscene gestures with my hand, and let them flutter down again. "You may use this as toilet paper," I said, and walked out. James did not translate, but this was one case where translation was not needed.

By this time, James had become a trusted friend. I told him we needed to find a factory that could be trusted to make products exclusively for us. James recommended a factory called Johnny Ru Machinery, where the boss was his personal friend. Johnny Ru manufactured large metalworking lathes for the American oil industry but had recently lost a contract from their largest customer. They had a huge facility, well-trained staff, and the equipment necessary to produce any kind of machinery.

Johnny Ru was willing to make woodworking machines for us exclusively, and ready to agree to our terms. James had a local Taiwanese attorney prepare the contract, which Johnny Ru promptly signed. This 1985 agreement was between James and Johnny Ru, since James was acting as a trading company and was technically the buyer.

Within a year, Johnny Ru was producing lots of various woodworking machines for us, which allowed us to sell our machines in the American market at a good price that others could not match. In fact, none of our competitors, or trading companies and other factories in Taiwan, even knew where these machines were being produced, since Johnny Ru was a metalworking-machinery factory and not known in the woodworking-machinery industry.

For a few years, things went great.

But about 1990, I started getting phone calls at night from Johnny Ru's English-speaking secretary, asking us to buy directly from them and cut out James. I told her this was impossible, since James was my friend and also had introduced me to them in the first place. But the secretary didn't give up, continuing to call almost weekly with the same request. I had to be diplomatic and polite while standing firm about keeping the existing relationships in place.

The calls went on for a year and then suddenly stopped. I commented to Leili that Johnny Ru must have finally accepted my refusal to cut out James and buy directly from them.

I was wrong. Johnny dear was planning something more sinister!

In 1992, I had just received my advance copies of woodworking magazines and was riffling through the first one when I saw an ad from a California company that looked suspiciously like our ads. I picked up another magazine, then another. The copycat ads were in all of them. We knew the magazine publishers really well, since we'd been advertising with them for years, and through them I found out the ads were being placed by a guy that went by the name YE and apparently had a relationship with a large factory in Taiwan. Further research yielded the alarming news that YE, who lived in Los Angeles, was the Johnny Ru boss's son-in-law.

Johnny Ru was embarking on a large-scale attack to take business from Grizzly and sell directly to the consumer themselves. They had a huge advantage as they were the factory!

They figured since Grizzly was selling so much, why not cut us out and take the extra profit themselves? In theory, that's a great model. In practice, there's a big difference between just offering a well-priced product versus offering a well-priced product via an efficient system that had been well-honed over time and had great after-service. With every new machine, you need a detailed instruction manual and exploded parts diagrams, with detailed information that's clear and concise. The manuals must be written in English with American safety precautions spelled out. Most of the so-called manuals that came from suppliers were no more than inadequate, poorly copied, badly written summaries. At Grizzly, we employed a team of technical writers and photographers who produced high quality manuals.

Other issues come into play, too. The machinery business requires lots of money to keep inventory in stock, and lots of warehouse space for bulky products. We had a full customer service department to handle customer calls and complaints, trained technicians who knew our machines to trouble-shoot over the phone, and a parts department to replace a part damaged in transit, overlooked at the factory, or just worn out.

I looked again at the copycat ads in the woodworking magazines. Magazine ads are not cheap, and this California company was spending money like a drunken sailor. Our supplier in Taiwan had indeed set up shop in the United States and was attempting to compete with us.

Never mind that they didn't have the pieces in place to run the business properly or the experienced staff that this business requires; we still needed to take action, fast. I told James there was no one in Taiwan that could be trusted to make machines exclusively for us. Therefore, he needed to make them himself! He knew all the subcontractors and suppliers, since he'd helped Johnny Ru set up for us.

James agreed, and started the process of buying a vacant factory and setting up production. During the year it took us and James to get into gear in Taiwan, we at Grizzly in the USA cut our prices to the bone to compete with Johnny Ru's California startup. That made it hard for them to sell their machines, which reduced their cash flow. Once we stopped buying from them, we began to hear via James that Johnny Ru was not paying their raw-materials suppliers in Taiwan. Next we got discreet information from magazines that they weren't getting paid for the California company's ads and had cut them off from future advertising.

For Grizzly, these two years were tough and trying times, but there was more at stake here than just one Taiwanese supplier competing on our home turf. I needed to show all present and future factories in Taiwan that if you encroach on my territory, I will fight back with all my might, losing money if I have to, to retain our market share.

It worked. In 1995, as quickly as Johnny Ru had started its operation in USA, it disappeared into the night. I learned later that the Johnny Ru boss and his wife had declared bankruptcy and vanished from Taiwan, leaving behind dozens of creditors who would never get paid.

Our skirmish with Taiwan was over. We had successfully repelled the attack. I was later told by another factory boss in Taiwan that all of the other factory bosses were watching to see what the outcome would be.

None ever ventured into the Bear's territory again.

CHAPTER 33

Goodbye Gorilla, Hello Elvis

Just because I didn't have a glass jaw did not mean my head wasn't reeling from the beating I absorbed after my outdoor-equipment venture Gorilla and Sons failed in 1996. After that debacle, I took a deep breath and renewed my focus on our main business of selling machinery and tools through Grizzly.

Grizzly's East Coast location in Williamsport, Pennsylvania was thriving, as was our West Coast headquarters in Bellingham. Both locations were in the northern part of the United States. It was time to seek a third location that could serve the Midwest as well the southern U.S., including large states such as Florida, Texas, and Arizona.

Memphis, Tennessee (where Elvis Presley lived most of his life) caught my attention. The road networks were good, and many companies were headquartered there, including FedEx. FedEx even had its own dedicated runway at the Memphis airport. Memphis in the mid-1990s was the nation's 18th largest city, with more than a million in population counting the surrounding suburbs.

Initial information from the Chamber of Commerce on available space, the labor market, and trucking terminals looked promising, so I flew to Memphis to meet with the Chamber as well as with other local leaders. They said hiring was easy, and the average hourly rate was lower than what we were paying in Bellingham and Williamsport. I found a 90,000 square-foot warehouse and signed a lease for three years. My goal was to rent for that period, and if the location worked out, we would construct our own building.

We would have existing managerial staff move from Williamsport to Memphis until such time as we could hire local managers. I had just the right folks in mind: Bill Shaffer and Debbie Eisner.

I first met Bill back in the early days of Williamsport, shortly after we'd opened that location in 1987. That day, I was working with our Williamsport general manager, Shirley Olsen (my very first employee when I started Grizzly) when I saw a tall, skinny young guy emptying garbage cans from under the desks of the office staff.

"Who's that?" I asked.

"Bill Shaffer," Shirley answered. "He comes into the offices twice a week to take out everybody's garbage."

I raised my eyebrows but said nothing. Everyone in the Bellingham offices, myself included, emptied our own trashcans. To this day, I can be seen in my suit, taking the little garbage container from under my desk to the 50-gallon trash can at the far end of the offices. But never mind, Shirley was in charge here, and she liked having Bill do this task.

As it turned out, young Bill was a hard worker at all tasks. Over the years he worked his way up to warehouse manager at Williamsport and was liked and respected by those who worked under him. (I strive, then and now, to reward and promote hard workers from within, and it's a point of pride for me that so many Grizzly employees have a long tenure with the company.)

By now Bill had turned into a solid young man; he was no longer the lanky kid I had met in Williamsport. Bill would run the new warehouse in Memphis. Debbie, another hard worker, who'd worked her way up from call center operator to a management position, would run the new showroom and offices.

We poured our heart and soul into the Memphis location. By now we had a fair amount of retail experience in product display, having created showrooms in Bellingham, Williamsport, and for Gorilla and Sons. From the type of slatwall wall coverings to rolling stands for power tools to simple things such as hooks, our Memphis showroom looked great and worked well.

Memphis also allowed us to centralize our parts department into one location. Our Bellingham parts supervisor, Jon Lamza, moved to Memphis. Other managers would make short visits, until we could hire more local managers.

But it turned out that it wasn't nearly as easy to hire staff as the Chamber had said. The best local employees were already working elsewhere and well paid; we couldn't compete with what FedEx was paying. We eventually were able to hire staff, but at 50 percent more than the average wage the Chamber had indicated.

In summer 1997, a few days before our grand opening, I went to Memphis and called a meeting with our new warehouse staff. We had hired twenty-five people locally, of which fifteen were warehouse workers, three would work in the parts department, and the rest were office and showroom staff. We met in our lunchroom, a big, square room furnished with tables and folding chairs. One by one the new warehouse guys, each one a strong-looking young black man, walked in, took a folding chair, and sat facing me.

Now, I was born in Africa of Indian parents and grew up with black friends and classmates. I played guitar in the school band with black bandmates. I never thought to judge anyone by their skin color, nor did they.

I stood, welcomed everyone, gave them a bit of background about our company, and spoke of my expectations for accuracy, hard work, and future plans. They listened to me with interest. Then I turned the meeting over to Bill, who was sitting five feet to my left, explaining why he'd moved to Memphis. Our business was specialized, and our processes had been perfected over many years; this launch required a manager with company experience. My expectation was that Bill would find workers who were motivated, train them in the Grizzly way, and eventually recommend one

193

for warehouse manager.

As I sat down and Bill took the floor, the expressions on the faces of our new workers grew hostile. With sudden alarm I thought, *"Ohhh--they don't like this white boy."*

I found out later Debbie had a similar experience with showroom and office staff.

We put that behind us and focused on the work ahead. Business was brisk, with customers coming from all over the region. Memphis was a metropolis with high population, which was good—but as we soon discovered, it was also a high crime area. We installed cameras in the showroom, and outside the building perimeter. We reinforced the doors. We installed sliding steel grates on the inside of the showroom windows, so people could still view our products during closed hours, but no one could break in. Our beautiful new showroom was starting to resemble the Elvis song "Jailhouse Rock." Business was rocking while we were inside the jailhouse!

More seriously, employee problems were escalating, with cash disappearing from the office and rampant cell phone use while driving forklifts. Bill would often find some of his workers sleeping among the warehouse racks. Outdoor security cameras were stolen—twice—despite having been installed fourteen feet off the ground. I did not replace them after the second time. Inside the warehouse, when the large overhead doors were raised for ventilation, thieves would run in, grab product, and dash out to a waiting car.

When our product was picked up from our Memphis warehouse to ship to customers, it would go first to a local main terminal for sorting, then to other terminals around the country. We found that 30 percent of the product that left our Memphis facility arrived damaged, and we traced this damage to Memphis' main terminal. We tried different shipping companies, but all had the same issues: the Memphis main terminal was known for damage to all kinds of products, not just ours.

Meanwhile, back in our own warehouse, employee problems continued. Jon Lamza in the parts department found one day that none of his three workers had shown up for work. Debbie and Bill, more than once, found feces smeared on our warehouse bathroom walls.

That was the beginning of the end. Unhappily, I set out to look for another location.

In January 1999, I bought a 15-acre parcel on the outskirts of Springfield, Missouri and within a few months had built a 150,000 square-foot building there. The Springfield city officials were pro-business, and our permitting and construction were completed less than six months from the day I purchased the land. We kept Memphis open just until Springfield was up and running. In the coming decades, we would find Springfield to be one of our company's best investments.

We closed Memphis eighteen months after our grand opening there. Once again, as with the Gorilla and Sons retail store in Bellingham, I paid rent for the remainder of the three-year lease. As they used to say in the concerts, Elvis had left the building!

In the midst of this, in 1998 I made the company-wide decision to change our company name from Grizzly Imports to Grizzly Industrial, as over the years we had been transitioning to a professional level of machinery, and now sold a lot of machines to manufacturers around the country. Also, in 1998, we opened our quality control office in Taiwan.

In 2020, as I write this memoir, I realize that my experience in Memphis may be uncomfortable for some readers, but as with other chapters, I remain honest in conveying what actually took place.

Shiraz in School Band

CHAPTER 34

Guns, Money, and the Internet

In the early days of the internet, almost no one knew what it was or how it worked. In 1993, newscasters still called it "an information superhighway" that offered "electronic mail addresses."

To remember what those days were like, consider the computer hardware setup in 1996 at Grizzly Industrial, an up-to-date and established company of about 150 employees then. We were using an IBM System/36 main computer, which served dedicated monitors placed around the offices. Some select staff also had personal computers on their desks, which did not communicate with the System/36.

I wasn't connected to the System/36, since I got whatever information I needed from it through my assistant, but I have always been an early adopter of technology once I understood what it could do, and I had a PC in my office. (In fact, back in 1983, I had been only the second company in all of Bellingham to buy one. I used my PC then with the Lotus 1-2-3 spreadsheet program that allowed me to input item costs and get month-end inventory values. I could have easily done that on the System/36, but I wasn't comfortable with others seeing costs of products early on in business. Of course, my thinking changed and with the security protocols available on the System/36, those functions were moved to it within a year or so.)

By the mid-1990s, the internet was gaining popularity. America Online, which later became AOL, was an early pioneer on the worldwide web, and its most recognized brand. You accessed it by dialing a desk-top phone using a modem. In 1996 American Online achieved five million members, many of whom were obtained through their mass mailings of floppy discs allowing people to see how easy it was to surf the web and meet people with similar interests.

I was one of those five million America Online members. Frankly, I thought America Online was the internet. After embarrassing myself during a discussion, I set out to learn how it worked. I found you could go to anyone's website if you had a website address, and almost all company website addresses ended in .com. I realized right away that there could only be one .com web address and once it was taken, you were out of luck. I knew immediately I should register Grizzly.com, but when I tried, I found it had already been taken. When I typed in Grizzly.com, the page showed a cryptic message saying that if I didn't understand the message, I was in the wrong place. It also had a password box.

I contacted the owner of this domain name, who turned out to be a professor of computer science at a university in California. He knew all about the internet before most people had even heard of it.

He was not interested in selling the domain name Grizzly.com.

I did the next best thing and registered grizzlyimports.com, and in 1996 we became the first machinery company to launch an internet website. It was a static website, meaning the viewer could find information and look at various products for sale, but couldn't interact with it or order anything online.

On the worldwide web back then, two search engines would crop up: Google, and Northern Light. Google was a funny name but easy to remember. Northern Light was thought to be innovative because it included both public and proprietary information sources. But when Northern Light tried to monetize what had been previously free, it started on a downward spiral, and soon no one remembered them.

Over the next six months, we saw traffic on grizzlyimports.com increasing. Many customers who phoned in mentioned information from our website. I wanted that short Grizzly.com name! I called the computer science professor in California and offered him $5,000 for the name. Back then, that was a lot of money for a domain name. I made the point that he wasn't doing anything with the Grizzly.com page—it was still showing only that single cryptic message.

He replied he was using the site for posting lessons and tests that his students could access via password. His answer was still no. He volunteered that his neighbor owned some Grizzly machinery and spoke highly of it. The professor offered to put a link to our site grizzlyimports.com on his Grizzly.com page, no charge.

That was a nice gesture and I accepted, but for me the uncertainty of him having the power to disconnect the link felt like an axe hanging over my head. He could pull the plug on me anytime. *Never mind,* I thought, *I'll contact him in six months and double my offer.*

I understood the value of domain names now, and I started registering other names associated with our products: planers.com, dustcollectors.com, bandsaws.com, etc. There were a few I couldn't get because somebody else had beaten me to it. As it turned out, a guy by the name of Garry Chernoff, who lived on Vancouver Island, was registering domains in every industry he could think of, and it seemed he was always one step ahead of me. Early on, folks like Garry were known as "cyber-squatters," but later they would become known as domain investors.

I would call Garry for a domain name occasionally, and I got to know him really well. He had a sense of humor. He'd quote a high price for a domain name, I'd call him a thief, and he'd laugh and come back with a similar insult. Garry told me there was another guy one step ahead of him, and he, Garry, sometimes struggled to get domain names.

Over the ensuing six months, we kept improving grizzlyimports.com and added more powerful servers.

It was time for my biannual call to the computer science professor in California, the owner of Grizzly.com. I now offered him $10,000, double my previous offer. I said if I owned the site, I would put a link on it for him.

His answer was a polite, firm "no." I was starting to feel helpless. There was nothing I could do!

While this was going on, I continued to register domain names associated with my industry. I also remained in contact with Garry Chernoff, bartering domain names with him. I accumulated more than 200 domain names related to our industry; it seemed everyone else in our industry was oblivious to this critical and fast-evolving technology.

Garry told me he owned SmithandWesson.com, and since I was interested in shooting, would I be interested in owning this name?

I replied Smith & Wesson was a very powerful gun company and wouldn't look kindly on anyone else owning their name. "You are a dead man, Garry," I joked, but added I'd take the risk if he wanted to give the domain name to me free.

"Free" was not in his vocabulary, Garry said, but since I was such a nice guy, he'd sell it to me cheap: $500.

SOLD! What Garry didn't know was that I held the worldwide licensing rights for Smith & Wesson tools. I had obtained those rights back in 1994-1996 when we were selling outdoor equipment through Gorilla and Sons. We sold a variety of specialty lighters bought from a distributor, and one of the brands was Smith & Wesson. We hadn't been selling them long when I got a call from John Steele, licensing director of Smith & Wesson, telling me we were infringing on their trademark.

I knew that all companies put a strong value on their patents and trademarks, also known as intellectual property. I also owned numerous trademarks and patents and knew how we would react if someone infringed on ours. I immediately stopped selling the lighters and pulled remaining product off the shelf, sending all infringing product to Steele, as he'd requested.

Steele was impressed with our response. We discussed the possibility of Grizzly Imports attaining the worldwide license for Smith & Wesson branded tools, and within a few months, we had signed a contract for that.

I would also later acquire the worldwide license for Smith & Wesson branded optics. John became a good business friend and we would talk every couple of months on the phone.

I knew someday their marketing department would wonder who owned SmithandWesson.com. They were currently using Smith.Wesson.com. Who is going to remember to put a dot between Smith & Wesson? What were they thinking?

But that was their problem. We got back to business and created a separate homepage for SmithandWesson.com displaying all the Smith & Wesson tools we were selling, and without being asked, added a link to their website.

It wasn't long before I got a call from John.

"Shiraz, you own SmithandWesson.com," John said.

"I do," I replied. "And I've added a link on it to your website."

"I saw that," he said. "I appreciate it."

I waited for him to ask more questions, but none came. All he said was that the S&W-licensed tools on our website looked good. That was the end of the conversation.

A few more months passed. John called again.

"Shiraz, you own SmithandWesson.com," John said.

"John, you said the same thing a few months ago."

"Yes," he said, clearing his throat. "Corporate would like to have that domain name."

I had known this day would come! I broke into a smile. I had bought it from Garry for $500 specifically for this day.

"John," I said, "it's yours."

"What?" John said. "What do you mean?"

"John, it's yours, free. It's a gift from me."

"What, you don't want anything for it?" John stumbled over the words. He acted as stunned as if someone had hit him with a baseball bat.

"No, you can have it," I said. "I hate to say this, John, but your marketing director is an idiot. What was he thinking, registering a domain name with a dot between names and leaving the real name out there for someone else to register?"

John was silent for a moment, holding the phone, taking this in.

"I have to give you something for it," he finally said. "Shiraz, you like guns, don't you? How about you pick out two guns from our Smith & Wesson custom shop, and I'll have them engraved for you?"

Oooh… that sounded delicious. I was not going to pass that up. I hadn't asked for anything, nor was I expecting anything.

"John, that would be great! Thank you!" I said.

"You know what," John continued, having regained his equilibrium, "pick out three guns and tell me what sort of engraving you'd like. I'll get it done."

I had paid only $500 for that name, which I'd recouped dozens of times over selling Smith & Wesson branded tools. But I was not about to look a gift horse in the mouth. Several months later, I received three custom-made Smith & Wesson pistols with heirloom engraving that normally would have cost $10,000 per gun.

Domain names often become an intellectual property battleground, but free heirloom guns?...Ho, ho, ho!!!

Smith & Wesson Heirloom Guns.

Three heirloom engraved guns presented as a gift from the
President of Smith & Wesson to Shiraz

A Bad Case of Capitalism

CHAPTER 35

Lawyers Should Be Lined Up And...

"Hey Shiraz, you want to buy Makita.com?"

It was good old Garry on the phone that day in 1998. Garry Chernoff was the domain investor who'd scooped up all sorts of names early on and could now peddle them at leisure.

Since we sold Makita-branded power tools at Grizzly, of course I was interested. I did think it odd that a big company like Makita didn't own Makita.com. Who lets stuff like that slip by? Another marketing genius who should've been fired.

Garry sold Makita.com to me for $500—a screaming deal—and right away we at Grizzly launched the Makita.com website for all Makita power tools that we sold, adding a link to Makitatools.com, which was Makita's website.

I fully expected to hear from Makita, but a year went by before I did.

We got that call via our local Makita sales rep, who said the company wanted that domain name. I replied that I'd invested a lot of money in graphics and web design to showcase the Makita products we bought from them, and I'd want to be reimbursed.

More months rolled by before I heard from the local rep again: the Japanese president of Makita North America wished to visit me.

A month later in April 1999, a black Lincoln town car rolled up to the front door of Grizzly on Valencia Street in Bellingham. Two American men exited the car, followed by a smaller Japanese man of middle age. I greeted the president with a slight bow, welcomed him to Grizzly, and presented a small gift, as is customary when dealing with Japanese. He also had a gift for me.

With my company vice president at my side, I led our guests through our showroom, past the bubbling fountain and reflecting pool to the curving staircase, flanked by two large wooden hand-carved grizzly bears, that leads up to our second-floor reception area and offices. Upstairs, I held open the heavy, polished wood door to our conference room and invited our guests in.

Our conference room is large and luxurious, with a coffered ceiling built of koa, a richly colored wood of varied grain available only from Hawaii. The walls are decorated with huge, artistic, framed maps of the world. The conference table, which seats fourteen, is made of bubinga, an African hardwood that's one of the more exotic woods in the world. The room is designed to impress and mentally disarm those entering for the first time.

The president took a seat on one side of the massive slab of bubinga, followed by his lieutenants on either side. I sat across from him, my VP next to me.

After small talk, the president got to the point. In accented English, he said they would like Makita.com back.

Though I knew what he meant, I responded by saying "Makita.com was never yours."

One of the American men quickly clarified that they wanted possession of Makita.com.

"And what is your position at Makita?" I asked.

The American puffed up a little as he answered that he was the company attorney.

I glanced at my VP with an expression that telegraphed, *these negotiations just went to hell.*

I turned back to the president, inquiring who his marketing guy was.

"I am," piped up the American on the other side of the president.

So this was the marketing genius who registered Makitatools.com, leaving Makita.com for someone else to register two years later. He was the reason Makita was in this fix. I looked at him a second longer, thinking it was no wonder Makita was the least aggressive in their marketing. Makita makes really good power tools, but their ads left a lot to be desired.

I said that I respected their position but had a great deal invested in the website and would need to be reimbursed.

The president responded cordially, and negotiations were off to a good start when Mr. Lawyer interrupted.

"Under the Lanham Act of 1946, as codified by section..." Blah, blah, blah. Mr. Lawyer finally ended his monologue with "...you cannot own this name because it is the name of our company."

I responded by saying that Makita is a generic Japanese name and there were dozens of other Makita-related sites already registered, and most of them did not even sell tools.

Then Mr. Lawyer did something very foolish. Instead of letting the president continue negotiations, he went for the jugular, adopting an aggressive tone and saying, "If you do not transfer this name to us within two weeks, we will sue you in court."

(There are good lawyers, average lawyers and very bad lawyers. Just because they went to law school and got a degree does not automatically give them logic. It didn't take any guesswork to figure out what category this guy was in. In my opinion, lawyers are a necessary evil. During an irritating matter on another subject I once told my lawyer here in Bellingham that all lawyers should be lined up and shot. She responded with "Oh dear." A couple of years later she went on to become a judge. Oops...)

Anyway, back to Mr. Lawyer from Makita. I looked at him, then looked at the Japanese president. I pushed back my chair and stood. My VP did the same. I held out my hand to the president, saying we appreciated his visit. The president looked bewildered and asked, haltingly, "What happened?"

I pointed at Mr. Lawyer. "He just threatened me," I said. "You should have left him at home."

The Makita contingent was still seated when we reached the conference room door.

As expected, a few days later I received a nasty-sounding letter from an outside firm representing Makita power tools. As I sat at my desk and read the letter, I laughed out loud. This was fun for me. What's the worst that could happen? I'd have to turn over a $500 name to them.

I responded to the attorney that I would fight this tooth and nail in court, they would likely lose, and when they did, I would plaster full-page ads about it in all the woodworking magazines.

They offered me $5,000 for the name. I countered with $50,000. We went back and forth for a few days until they said $30,000 was their final offer and I had until 3 p.m. that day, Friday, to respond before they filed a lawsuit.

I told them I absolutely had to have $35,000 and they had until 5 p.m. to reply. I added that come Monday morning, my price would go back to $50,000, and that it would cost them much more than that to litigate it.

Later that afternoon I received a fax from them saying they were accepting my offer and would pay $35,000.

I didn't tell them that I would have sold Makita.com to them for less than half of that final price, had Mr. Lawyer not taken an abrasive attitude with me.

Conference Room at Grizzly Headquarters

CHAPTER 36

Boo Koo Bucks for You, Professor

In the matter of Makita.com, I had the upper hand. Not so with Grizzly.com. That name, which I badly wanted, was still the property of a computer science professor at a California university, who was using it as a lesson-and-testing platform for his students. My last offer to him for that domain name had been $10,000, which he'd refused.

A few months later I offered him $20,000. That was a huge amount back then for a name, but I knew what I wanted to do with it; I had big plans. Once again, his answer was a polite "no," but to pacify me he said that if he were ever to sell the domain name Grizzly.com, it would be to me.

I was getting deeply annoyed but there was absolutely nothing I could do. Not too many things bothered me, but this situation really did. I felt helpless, watching the internet gaining in popularity by the day.

A few months later, I took another run at him, doubling my offer again to $40,000 for Grizzly.com. He said "no" once again. Now I was angry--at myself, because I was negotiating with myself, and because it felt like I was talking to a wall.

By late 1999, website activity for all companies, not just ours, was increasing at a breakneck pace. Grizzly was the name of my company, a short name that is easily remembered. I could not force the California professor to sell Grizzly.com to me via legal action as it was a generic animal name and anyone could own it.

The internet promised a rate of growth and success unimaginable just a few years before, and Grizzly was well-positioned to take advantage of it, if only I had that name. Internally, it almost felt like I was emulating a child throwing a tantrum for a new toy! We had opened our Taiwan office in 1998 and embarked on a program to improve the overall quality of our machines with better components and better control during manufacturing. We had hired several engineers on the Grizzly payroll who worked in our Taiwan office. In Bellingham, we had transitioned from outside programming services to an in-house IT department. We'd hired the best programmers, who worked primarily on our website enhancements.

We wanted to make our site totally interactive and enable customers to order online. There were no cookie-cutter programs available that could handle all the nuances of our business, so all code had to be written from scratch.

I could visualize the coming impact of the fast-evolving internet era on business and commerce, but to keep up with it and achieve what I wanted, I needed that name!

I wanted to have special nameplates made with Grizzly.com. All of our print ads, our catalogs, our spec labels on machines, and our manuals would have Grizzly.com plastered all over them. If someone saw a machine anywhere, they did not have to wonder who made it--they would see Grizzly.com clearly on the machine. I was thinking long-term: ten years, twenty, thirty, more. With the internet growing so fast, a marketing effort based on Grizzly.com would do wonders for the future of our business.

This computer science professor had rebuffed me so many times, I wanted to pull my hair out. He didn't need Grizzly.com but was keeping it to run a class. He could have done that with any domain name. It was so frustrating!

Finally, I said to myself, screw this! I would make him an offer that only a fool would refuse. I offered him $200,000, telling him that if he refused my offer, I would walk away forever and use that $200,000 for other marketing on grizzlyimports.com. This was my final and last run at Grizzly.com.

He responded instantly. He said he was at an internet café in Hamburg, Germany. He accepted my offer and added that I had made his day.

Many people at the time thought I paid too much for the name but considering that we do tens of millions of dollars' worth of business every year on Grizzly.com, that $200,000 turned out to be one of my best and most precious investments.

That year, 2000, we also opened our Shanghai office. I promptly hired Cindy, the engineer who'd been my contact in China when I bought Dollar Trading Company back in 1993, to run it.

In Bellingham, our in-house IT department grew busier by the day. With Grizzly.com now in our possession, we were poised to grow as fast as the internet would let us.

As the years would go by, we would maintain our position on the cusp of the internet cutting edge, several years ahead of our competitors.

Machine with Grizzly.com

Buildings with grizzly.com

CHAPTER 37

Expansion and Recession Simultaneously

With Grizzly.com in hand, we unleashed a slew of marketing, plastering Grizzly.com wherever we could, on our website, machinery, manuals, print and digital advertising, and in gigantic letters on the side of our buildings in Bellingham, Springfield, and Williamsport.

Once again, business was booming. The 150,000-square-foot building we'd built on our 15-acre parcel in Springfield in 1999 for a large showroom and national distribution of our products was quickly filling up. This building had a large parking lot, but we needed that area for our huge annual Tent Sale, which attracted thousands of people for a day-long extravaganza of bargains.

Across the street was a vacant 40-acre parcel. My realtor had told me the owner, an older gentleman, had considered selling it for $1 million a couple of years before but then withdrawn it for unknown reasons. At my request, my realtor contacted him now, but his reply was "not for sale."

I phoned him up myself. The owner, eighty years old and sharp, said he was leaving the property to his three adult children in his will.

"It is their future," he said simply.

"As a father myself, I understand that," I said. "But for the sake of discussion, if you were to sell it, what might its price be?"

He paused. I waited.

"Somewhere in the neighborhood between two and three million," he answered.

That was nearly triple what he had quoted the realtor a couple years prior, but this property was critical to our future expansion. Plus, a property about half as big, a block away, had just sold for over $2 million. We chatted briefly about other things, establishing rapport, before I thanked him and left it at that.

I wanted to be courteous and transparent, so two weeks later I phoned him again. He appreciated being approached directly but was adamant about leaving the forty acres to his heirs.

"You can probably buy it from them," he told me.

"Yes, but I'd have to wait for you to die," I replied, "and on the phone you sound like a young man."

He laughed.

Any negotiation involves multiple options, and I'd been thinking about this one from his point of view. His goal was to care for his kids. I asked if he knew what his kids planned to do with the property after they inherited. He didn't.

I had a pretty good idea what they'd do with it. "Usually, heirs spend inheritances buying new cars and boats, upgrading things around the house, taking deluxe trips, and pretty soon the money's gone," I said. "But if you sold the property to me now and used the proceeds to open three trusts, and specified how the trusts were to invest, they'd have continuous income and you could preserve the asset for them even after you're gone."

He liked that, and within weeks we had a deal at $3 million. Immediately upon possession in 2000, I built a 300,000-square-foot warehouse on it, leaving plenty of room for another million square feet of warehouse space to be built in the future, if needed.

Once again, though initially expensive, this turned out to be a killer deal. It wouldn't be long before the city of Springfield would expand out past our facilities. The unbuilt balance of that parcel is now worth much more than what I paid for the whole forty acres. Of course, it won't be sold because it's set aside for long-term expansion of Grizzly Industrial.

While all this was happening, we also purchased twenty-two acres of land near a mall in Muncy, Pennsylvania, fifteen minutes away from our existing Williamsport location. In 2001 we built a 220,000-square-foot building on it, moved our Pennsylvania operations in, and sold the building in Williamsport--the one we had purchased as a shell building from the City of Williamsport in 1986. Now we had all the infrastructure—domain name, land and building in Springfield, and a bigger, new building in Muncy, to grow our business. We were on a roll!

Instead, the economy rolled into recession, ending the longest expansion on record in the United States. Experts said later that the economy might have been able to avoid the Recession of 2001 if not for the additional hit of the Sept. 11, 2001 terrorist attacks. That horrific event changed the world, and also all but shut down the U.S. economy for several days.

In the Recession of 2001, all types of companies that were heavily leveraged had a hard time, and many folded. Luckily, Grizzly was in a strong financial position, as we'd been investing profits back into the company to reduce our dependency on banks. No business leader likes giving banks financial power over his company; my opinion of banks was no better than my opinion of lawyers. When the sun is shining, banks are happy to hold an umbrella over your head. As soon as it starts raining, they yank that umbrella!

Meanwhile, I saw what was happening to overseas factories, including our manufacturers in Taiwan. As customer orders dried up, they didn't have enough work for their employees or enough money to pay their bills. Some were teetering on the brink of closing down. That would be a big problem long-term for us, as we needed our orders filled. I began placing orders with various factories, even though we didn't need the product right away, to keep the factories alive. It worked, and as a side benefit, we garnered a tremendous amount of loyalty and respect from them.

At home in the United States, unemployment spiked, and kept rising through 2003. As workers were laid off across the country, many wanted to create an income by producing cabinets and other woodworking items. Their purchasing dollars were limited, and so these customers gravitated toward Grizzly. Most other companies that offered woodworking machinery sold through distributors and dealers, creating layers of increased cost between manufacturer and end-user. Because our sales model was direct to consumer, our selling price for a similar item was much lower. Customers turned to us.

During that time, a couple of our smaller competitors went out of business, and some of our larger competitors saw their sales drop 20 to 40 percent. Our sales, during that hard Recession of 2001, increased by more than 20 percent. All that additional product we had ordered from overseas manufacturers to keep them busy actually came in handy, to fulfill new business pouring in. Likewise, our new warehouses in Springfield and Muncy, opening on the eve of the recession, helped us cope with the storage and processing of the additional product that came in.

Later, economists would decree that the Recession of 2001 was relatively short, lasting only about eight months. But to businesses that lived through it, it felt much longer. For many companies, its negative effects were disastrous.

Looking back, we at Grizzly felt fortunate to experience expansion during a time of recession.

Aerial View of Missouri Warehouses

A Bad Case of Capitalism

CHAPTER 38

Good Cop, Bad Cop: Feds in my Home

I am an avid target rifle shooter, but the pace of business throughout the late 1990s left me nearly no time for my beloved hobby. Those years of closing Gorilla and Sons, opening and closing Memphis, diving into the internet revolution, purchasing Grizzly.com, opening our Taiwan and Shanghai offices, building new facilities in Springfield and Muncy—the late 1990s were a blur of 12- to 14-hour days, at least six days a week.

I kept my membership in Bellingham's Plantation Rifle Range though I rarely had time to use it. Plantation is a beautiful 300-yard rifle range, perfectly flat and well maintained by the County. I had joined that range upon moving to Bellingham in the early 1980s. Early on, I would practice there almost every weekend. Over the years, I'd won many 300-yard local matches. I had several custom-made rifles built for me that were extremely accurate. I did all my own reloading (making my own ammunition), which was a prerequisite to shoot very accurately for competitions.

It was common knowledge that I liked and owned guns, and that was no problem.

Then the terrorist attacks on Sept. 11, 2001 threw the country into turmoil.

On Nov. 7, 2001, less than two months after 9/11, my wife Leili had just wrapped up a visit with me at my office and was headed down the curving staircase at Grizzly headquarters in Bellingham as two unknown burly men in suits and ties were headed up.

They saw Leili and whipped out their badges. "Stop right there," they said to my wife.

Leili is a strong-willed person who takes no nonsense from anyone. That includes officials flashing badges. Unflustered, manners intact, she said to the men, "Go see my husband." Without pausing, she pointed up toward my office and continued down the stairs.

The two men looked at each other. They weren't used to having requests ignored, however politely. But Leili was continuing through the showroom toward the front door. The men had two options: sprint after and tackle her or carry on upstairs to see me.

Wisely, they chose the latter.

The two men announced themselves as special agents with the Department of the Treasury's Bureau of Alcohol, Tobacco, and Firearms the moment they walked into my office, leaving our receptionist no time to let me know I had visitors.

"We are here to ask you a few questions," said the bigger one in an aggressive tone as both flashed their badges again.

"Hello, gentlemen," I said as I assessed the two men. The bigger man had a small scar on his left cheek and a strong jaw that made him look like the Bad Cop. The other guy, about an inch shorter and ten years older, kept a smile plastered on his face: Good Cop. I got a gut feeling that Good Cop was more dangerous.

I stayed calm. "If you two will please take a seat, I'll go ask Don, my vice president here at Grizzly, to join us. I will need someone present to observe and witness whatever it is you are going to do here today."

Don, quickly summoned by our receptionist, entered. I introduced him and he quickly took a seat.

Good Cop began, speaking smoothly, his smile not budging. "Do you own any guns?"

"Yes, I do."

"Where do you shoot?"

"I haven't had time to shoot lately," I said, "but when I do, I go to the Plantation Rifle Range here in Bellingham. I have a yearly pass there."

"Do you keep any cordite at home?" Good Cop went on.

"What's cordite?" I had no idea.

"It's gunpowder," Bad Cop said.

I told them I kept gunpowder at home to make ammunition for my target practice.

"How much?" Bad Cop asked curtly.

"It's been a while since I've done any reloading, but I would guess I have eight to twelve pounds," I said. "Look, guys, you haven't told me why you're here and why you're interested in my shooting."

Bad Cop took the lead in responding and was straightforward with answers. He said one of my neighbors in Bellingham had driven to the FBI office in Seattle, ninety miles away, alerting them there was a Muslim with guns in the house behind his. The neighbor had told them he was sure I had a shooting range in my house and was "up to no good."

I laughed out loud. "There's nothing sinister about me. I'm a well-known businessman in town. Shooting has been my long-time hobby, and I don't have a range in my house."

Bad Cop continued that since the neighbor's report involved guns, the BATF took over the investigation from the FBI. Good Cop said they had already checked with the chief of the Bellingham Police Department, which had no record of me breaking the law. Not even a traffic ticket.

"Would you allow us to check your home so we can conclude this matter?" Good Cop asked nicely.

I was pretty sure this was not a request. "On one condition," I responded. "Our house is a no-shoes home, and you'll have to remove your shoes before coming inside.

They agreed. It turned out that they'd already been to my home that morning, but since they found no one at home except the security guy, they'd come to Grizzly.

We drove to my house, my vice president Don still with us. I let everyone in, and they took off their shoes in the foyer. As soon as we walked into the

223

main living room, Good Cop handed me a document to sign.

"It's a consent form that allows us to search your home, and if we find anything illegal, we can use that as evidence against you in a court of law."

Whoa! I had thought I would allow them to search my home as a courtesy. I wanted to help them get done with me so they could spend their time investigating actual threats to our country. But this consent form cast everything in a new and unwelcome light. I knew I could refuse them, but that would infer some kind of guilt that I had something to hide.

I glanced at Don. His look said *Go ahead and sign it.*

Good Cop and Bad Cop were watching me intently. I pulled out my pen and signed.

Their search took a couple of hours. They started in the main room, reading the titles of books on the bookshelf. They paused at a framed photo of our son.

"Who's this?" Bad Cop said, his aggressive tone returning.

I replied that was my son Shabir. They pressed further, asking where he lived. "Next door," I said.

They wanted to see my reloading area and looked at all the equipment without touching anything. They had zero interest in the gunpowder I had on the shelf. I opened my gun safe and showed them my rifles and pistols. They didn't speak, but their expressions showed they appreciated the quality of the guns. Bad Cop commented on one of my particularly nice target rifles, saying he'd never seen one like that.

One by one, they picked up and checked every gun.

I hadn't opened the safe or handled any of my guns for so long, and since I had nothing to fear from their investigation, I started to enjoy looking at my guns again. Each one brought back happy memories of the competitions and awards, of the days when I'd had time for regular target practice.

They checked the contents of every toolbox in my reloading room, and then we descended to the basement. This was where my "got nothing better to do" neighbor thought I had a shooting range. It was actually my workshop, filled with woodworking and metalworking machines. I have always been a hobbyist user of the machines my company sells.

Good Cop and Bad Cop loosened up as they started ogling the machines. "I wish I had room in my house for this sort of thing," Bad Cop said.

"Me, too," Good Cop said. "Look at this machine over here. What is it, and how do you use it?" I told them how a milling machine is used, and as we chatted, they relaxed a little more.

They went on to check the entire house. Satisfied that nothing was illegal, Good Cop handed me his business card and told me he appreciated my cooperation. "If anybody gives you any trouble, have them contact me," he said.

I tucked the card in my breast pocket as we walked back upstairs. "I understand that you're just doing your jobs," I said. "I realize it's nothing personal."

They put on their shoes at the front door, and Don and I waved them off.

The whole episode actually created a happy outcome: handling my guns made me realize how long it'd been since I'd had time to shoot. It gave me the initiative to start shooting and competing again.

And did I ever!

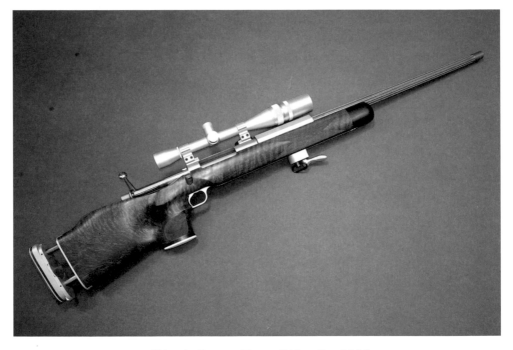

Shiraz's Custom Target Rifle - Pre 2000

CHAPTER 39

Drama on the Range

After the interesting visit from the special agents of the Bureau of Alcohol, Tobacco, and Firearms, the very next weekend in autumn 2001 I was back at the Plantation Rifle Range in Bellingham.

Business had kept me away too long! My interest in the sport had never waned, but I returned to it now with renewed focus, and over the next couple of years, I won most of the competitions in my category at the range. Since I used a scope on my rifle, I was in the "Any Rifle, Any Sight" category.

I soon heard of a new category called F-Class, newly accepted by the National Rifle Association, where the competitor shoots long distance from a prone position with a rifle propped on a rest out in front. The F comes from the name of the man who came up with the idea years before, Canadian George Farquharson. The shooter lays in the prone position on the ground, on a mat, and shoots with a scoped rifle using a front rest to support the rifle, very much like a sniper. I switched to this category, which soon became the fastest-growing class in the shooting world. I started winning the 300-yard F-Class matches at Plantation, as well as a couple of Washington State championships.

I called up the captain of the U.S. F-Class shooting team, Eric Bair, and asked to join the team. He asked what distance I shot at. When I answered 300 yards, he laughed.

"The U.S. team shoots at 1,000 yards," Eric said. "Compete in some of these matches. If you can shoot well at 1,000 yards, then we'll talk."

I had never shot that distance, and there were no 1,000-yard ranges anywhere near me. I didn't even know what kind of rifle and caliber were required. I started scouring forums for information and asking questions. Soon, I found out that you pretty well have to take information on the forums with a grain of salt because everyone is a "keyboard expert." However, there was one person by the name of Bob Pastor, who had proven himself as a good shooter and won many matches, who guided me to have a rifle built with a custom caliber.

I started practicing with the new rifle, and a few months later, I entered the 2006 U.S. F-Class national championship in Sacramento, California, comprised of around 150 shooters, including most of the U.S. team. Bob Pastor was there, giving me pointers on practice day.

This was the first time I'd competed at 1,000 yards--in fact, the practice day was the first time I had ever shot at 1000 yards. I placed 11th nationally, beating many U.S. team members. Bob, who placed 12th, was pleased for me. U.S. team captain Eric Bair won that match. A few months later, I shot at a 1,000-yard match in Tullahoma, Tennessee. I came in second, beating Bair and every other member of the U.S. team present. After that, I was quickly recruited to the U.S. team.

The U.S. team function is to gather the best shooters in the country and compete at the F-Class World Championships, held once every four years in a host country. The next one would be in England in 2009.

A year after Sacramento, at the 2007 F-Class national championship in New Mexico, the new U.S. team captain, Bob Bock, offered me the position of vice captain, which I gladly accepted. He knew I had the resources to help run the team. I welcomed the opportunity, but I had no idea of the challenge I would face from the captain of another U.S. Team.

F-Class is divided into two categories. F-T/R (for standard Target rifle) and F-Open. It's similar to other sports where you have a stock category, and an unlimited or Open category. Both are shot from the prone position but involve different calibers and front rests. Open allows a larger variety of calibers that can be "loaded hot" for maximum performance. Bob Bock was captain of the U.S. F-Open team; a shooter named Drake was captain of the F-T/R Team.

Bob Bock put me in charge of uniforms (hats and shirts with an embroidered emblem) for both teams. I searched the internet for red, white, and blue shirts. None were readily available; they would need to be custom ordered, take months to arrive, and were expensive as well. The shirt colors that were available in the marketplace were a dark navy (almost black) and white, since these were the colors our U.S. Olympic team had just used.

I emailed Bob about the scarcity of red, white, and blue shirts, including a link to the classy navy-and-white ones. Bob asked me to send Drake the information and let him know this was the choice for uniforms.

Drake emailed back to me, "I don't know what country's colors you aspire to, but I aspire to red, white, and blue."

I could not let that pass. I blasted Drake for his ignorance and bigotry and forwarded a copy to Bob Bock. I told Drake he was not my captain, and any future communication to me should go through Bob. I found out later Bob also had words with Drake about this. Drake later apologized, but the damage to our relationship had been done.

Both teams ended up going with the navy-and-white shirts I'd originally chosen. At the World Championships in England, our U.S. team took the silver medal overall. I was also a shooter on the four-man international team that took gold in that event.

But more drama lay ahead.

Shiraz Shooting Prone F-Class

CHAPTER 40

Ignorance and Bigotry Self-Destruct

The election was coming up. Not the U.S. presidential election, but an election for captain of the U.S. shooting team. I put my name in the hat, but a shooter named Brian was chosen.

Brian immediately asked me to be his vice-captain. I declined, saying the team had spoken.

Shortly after, at the next national championships, Brian took me out for dinner and asked me again to be his vice-captain, pretty much telling me he couldn't run the team without my help. Once again, I advised him to choose someone else.

Brian, who worked for an international IT firm and spent much of his time on global business travel, said he didn't really have the time required to run the team but had put his name in the ring at the urging of several team members. I finally agreed to his request--if I were given complete autonomy and not have to vet team communication through him. He agreed, and once again I became vice-captain of the U.S. team.

It turned out that Brian had even less time than he'd expected, and I wound up doing most of the work of running the team. Brian told me he was thinking of giving up his captain position and turning the team over to me.

At the next national championship match, I was standing on the shooting line during a ceasefire when two fellow team members walked up to me, took me aside, and said they had something to talk about. It seemed another team member, Rod, was deeply disturbed that I was vice-captain of the team.

I knew Rod, though I purposely limited my interaction with him. He was one of those people who talked nonstop, which is tedious for anyone unlucky enough to be in conversation with him, or around him. The two team members said Rod was gabbing about how I was probably not an American citizen, that only citizens should be on the team, that he had a friend who worked for the U.S. Department of Homeland Security, and he was going to get this friend to check up on me. Apparently, Rod kept on talking—no surprise—and said I likely couldn't even speak English.

I laughed out loud at the stupidity of it all but thanked my two teammates for their concern. In my mind I thought, *he is a few years late--Homeland Security has been there, done that.*

That evening, the thirty of us gathered for a regular team meeting. I was seated at the head table next to Brian, facing everyone. Brian opened by saying he was stepping down, and I would be taking over as captain of the team. Aware that I was not the team's first choice, I stood and addressed the team.

"If anyone does not want me as captain, speak now, because I don't want to be your captain if you don't want me," I said. I paused, then said, "If any of you want to be captain, now's the time to speak up."

Silence. Then Bob Bock, who'd been captain before Brian, stood. "When I was captain, Shiraz was a great help as my vice-captain," Bob said. "I couldn't have fulfilled all the obligations of being captain without him."

Two coaches on the team stood next, each saying they recommended me as captain.

Rod was present but remained quiet as a church mouse. Perhaps he was in shock that I could speak English.

There were no objections, and I became captain of the U.S. team. The next day, out on the shooting range, one of my teammates asked if I would kick Rod off the team now. I said no, everyone would get a fair chance to make the final cut, but Rod was an inconsistent shooter and would likely self-destruct. "Everyone's shooting will speak for them, and we'll take the best," I said. "However," I continued, "if he becomes disruptive on the team, I will boot his ass off the team."

Sure enough, when the final scores were tallied, Rod was at the bottom and did not make the cut.

Our team took silver again at the World Championships that were held for the first time in the USA in Raton, New Mexico in 2013.

Over the years, personally I did well at long range 1,000-yard shooting, having won three Canadian F-Class National championships, and numerous gold medals at national matches including being a four-time champion of the USA four-man-team event as well as winning several other international matches. In 2017, I earned the ultimate medal: International Distinguished Rifleman, given by the NRA to the best shooters in the USA who performed exemplarily in international matches.

After the 2013 World Championships, I ended my captaincy of the U.S. team, but I remain a dedicated and active member of the team, and I look forward to competing in the next World Championships.

Team Grizzly - United States 1000 Yd. National Champions
Our coach, Trudie Fay (center) is an amazing wind reader. I call her "Queen Bee"
Front Row: Emil Kovan, Queen Bee, John Myers
Back Row: Shiraz, David Mann

Distinguished Medal

Distinguished Rifleman Certificate

CHAPTER 41

Dirty Tricks by the Competition

I f business were easy, it would not be fun.

The years from 2006 to 2010 were jam-packed with excitement, including my activity on the U.S. shooting team, the Great Recession of 2007 to 2010, our purchase of an additional eleven acres in Muncy, Pennsylvania, construction of a 190,000-square-foot warehouse there— and a dirty trick played on us by Jet Tools, an old competitor of Grizzly.

Jet's early businesses included metalworking machinery as well as tools and accessories for the tool rental market such as jacks, hoists, etc. As years went by, Jet entered the woodworking machinery business and started buying these products from Taiwan. They entered this market several years after Grizzly. Jet sold through dealers who would then sell to end-users; with that extra layer of profit for the middleman, their retail prices were much higher than ours, since we sold direct to consumer. At every turn, we seemed to be in their face: their customers were constantly asking them why their machines were so much more expensive than Grizzly's. Jet dealers had a hard time explaining the price difference for what was, in many cases, an identical machine. Instead, the dealers resorted to the predictable response of badmouthing Grizzly machines as being supposedly inferior quality.

My motto has always been "never badmouth the competition" because then you're advertising for them while not promoting the merits of your own product. When customers called Grizzly, our customer-service agents spoke only about Grizzly machinery. On the other hand, low-level salespeople at dealers around the country that sold Jet and other branded machines badmouthed Grizzly. This generally backfired as they were indirectly sending customers to us!

Many of Grizzly's machines had a two-tone color scheme: tan and green. Our Woodstock machinery, sold under the Shop Fox brand, was off-white. Jet's machines were cream-colored, and they had trademarked the color White with the United States Patent and Trademark Office, including a description of all cream and beige colors. Boggles my mind how they received a trademark for that. I felt this was no more than a feel-good trademark without teeth; such a thing couldn't really be enforced since so many white, off-white, beige, and similar machines of other brands had been in the marketplace for decades.

At a tradeshow in Las Vegas in 2007, I discovered Jet would attempt to use this to play their dirty trick on us.

The AWFS Fair is the largest tradeshow for woodworking equipment on the West Coast. Grizzly had a 5,000-square-foot booth there with dozens of machines on display, and Woodstock had a 1,000-square foot booth; both were generating interest from all sorts of potential customers when three men in suits walked toward the Grizzly booth. One of them, a smaller man, was pointing at several of our machines. I saw the butt of a pistol inside the open suit jacket of one of the bigger men.

The three approached me. I was wearing a suit, so they likely thought I was someone important. I asked if I could help them.

The bigger man said they were from the Department of Homeland Security, enforcement division, then nodded at the smaller man who'd been pointing at our machines, introducing him as the attorney for Jet. He inquired who I was, and when I replied I was president of the company, he asked me to come upstairs to the show office with them.

I asked my vice president, Don, to come with us. Upstairs, with the five of us seated in a conference room, the bigger guy from Homeland Security enforcement—the one with the pistol in his suit jacket—started rattling legalese about trademark infringement and said we were infringing on Jet's white trademark color. He said that it was their job to enforce trademark infringers from bringing product into the United States.

I responded that woodworking machines had been produced in white for decades, long before Jet started selling them. "There is a sea of white machines on the show floor below, being offered by many different exhibitors," I pointed out.

"It doesn't matter if other companies are also infringing," he said. "If several drivers on a highway are speeding, but we catch only one, he's still speeding." He told me they would be confiscating certain machines from both the Grizzly and Woodstock booths, and we would not be allowed to display them.

He handed me a long list with our model numbers, but fortunately for us, we were displaying newer models that had different model numbers, except for a few machines that they indeed quickly removed off the floor.

This was Jet's dirty trick, attempting to force us to have an empty booth at a major show while they probably gloated about it in their own booth a few hundred yards away.

But while my VP and I were still in that upstairs conference room, I had phoned Grizzly's intellectual property attorney in Chicago. By that afternoon, our IP guy had gotten the Supreme Court of the United States, in an emergency hearing, to issue a temporary restraining order on Homeland Security's ability to confiscate our machines.

Boy, those two Homeland Security officers were not happy when we delivered the court order to them to release our machines that evening!

Next morning, our machines were back in place in our booth.

That was hardly the end of the saga that began that day in 2007 in Vegas. In fact, it was just the beginning of what would become a years-long, nasty legal battle.

The temporary restraining order our IP attorney achieved that day via the Supreme Court's emergency hearing only lasted two weeks. When it expired, Homeland Security started confiscating all of our shipping containers that came into every port in the country. This was a huge problem, because without product, we were out of business. We had to have all the containers moved, at our expense, to a bonded warehouse, unload them, and then transport only our machines that were solid green in color onto trucks headed to our warehouses. We were forced to leave the rest of our product behind in the bonded warehouse, incurring a daily storage charge. It was expensive and seriously disruptive.

Even the U.S. Customs team we were dealing with in Seattle thought the situation was ridiculous. In fact, one of the officers said so to us in a phone call and must also have voiced this to a superior, because he was promptly transferred!

The Washington, D.C. office of Homeland Security kept firing pointed directives at us. I could not understand why so much effort was being put into this issue. We found out later that Jet had hired a high-profile attorney in Washington whose office just happened to be on the same floor as Homeland Security's enforcement division headquarters.

We fought it out in court in Chicago. My personality is such that if I feel I'm being unjustly accused, and have done nothing wrong, I will fight back, no matter the cost. We eventually won an injunction against having our containers grabbed, valid until the case was resolved.

We had a strong defense against Jet's ridiculous attack. Unknown to Jet, I had saved all the magazines we'd advertised in since our inception in 1983, storing them in our warehouse pallet racking. Our managers scoured those magazines, pulling out dozens of ads by different companies selling white and off-white machines long before Jet was even selling woodworking machines.

The case dragged on for years, costing both parties millions in legal fees, probably them more than us, as they had a whole team of outside attorneys who kept pouring gas on the fire to increase billable hours. I had to assume that Jet's Swiss parent company started seeing those huge legal fees and instructed them to end the case.

While we were unable to recoup any of our legal bills and losses from the disruption, I celebrated its end by coming out with a new line of beautiful pure white machines. I called it the Polar Bear series.

Now there were two ferocious bears on the attack in the marketplace… growl, grrr!

2011 Grizzly Catalog Cover Introducing the Polar Bear Series of Machines

Polar Bear Series Logo

CHAPTER 42

The Great Recession and the Icon

I have always admired South Bend Lathe Works, an industry icon that's made top-quality metalworking lathes since the early 1900s. Back in 1975 and 1976, when I was buying used metal-cutting lathes to fix and sell, I came across many old South Bend lathes. In those days, working in the small area carved out next to the side door of the dry-cleaning store in Vancouver, B.C., I got to see the innards of the old, used machines as I took them apart to repair them. The quality of South Bend lathes was amazing compared to other machines I'd repaired.

South Bend Lathe Works was founded by Irish immigrants and identical twins John and Miles O'Brien in South Bend, Indiana in 1906. Within twenty-five years, they had become the largest manufacturer of metalworking lathes in the world. At one point, they owned two-thirds of the worldwide supply of metalworking lathes and had customers in eighty-eight countries. Their machines were used in shop classes of major universities and colleges throughout the country. Every U.S. Navy ship that rolled out of the shipyards had at least one South Bend lathe on it.

Over the years, as Grizzly was evolving into a major player in the machinery industry, South Bend Lathe Works was undergoing changes of its own. The O'Brien brothers had passed on, and their company had had several changes of ownership as well as other management issues. It was eventually purchased by a company that would take orders for lathes only on a custom-order basis, delivering the machines several months later. They also supplied parts for the machines that'd been sold over the past hundred years.

I hated to see this iconic brand put on the back burner compared to other brands in the industry. In 2006 I asked the owners if they would sell the company to me. They refused. I kept calling, every six months or so, even as the housing crisis was tipping the country into what would become the Great Recession of 2007 to 2010.

We had had several recessions over the past decades. Grizzly had lived through two of them, and actually grown during them. But none compared to the magnitude of the Great Recession that came at us full force in 2007. Grizzly and Woodstock had built up a war chest to reduce our dependency on banks. Remember how I said banks will hold an umbrella over your head only when the sun is shining? At Grizzly we had our own umbrella that we kept over our heads year-round, to shield us from anything the economy might rain down.

But the Great Recession threw down thunderstorms. By some accounts, 1.8 million small businesses went belly-up, unemployment rose to more than 10 percent, and billions of dollars evaporated from all sorts of companies as well as households. It would become the worst economic and financial meltdown since the Great Depression of the 1930s. Some of our competitors got "drenched," losing as much as 50 percent of their sales.

Despite the strong financial umbrella we always held over our heads, we got our feet wet. Our business was down 25 percent at its lowest point in 2010, before it turned around and surged up again.

We are proud that we were able to maintain almost all employees during the Great Recession. Workers in manufacturing industries that relied heavily on external financing were most likely to lose their jobs during this time, according to the Federal Reserve. Our umbrella helped us avoid that! Our financial strength also allowed us, as in past recessions, to continue to place orders with factories overseas so they could remain open and allow us uninterrupted supply into the future.

Those years were busy with the Jet lawsuit, the U.S. shooting team activity, and the 2008 purchase of land and construction of a 190,000-square-foot warehouse in Muncy, Pennsylvania, which brought our total warehouse space in Pennsylvania to 420,000 square feet. Through it all, I kept calling the owners of what was now called the South Bend Lathe Company. Finally, one day in 2009, perhaps because of financial reasons in their other ventures, they decided to sell the company.

The acquisition of this industry icon was a feather in my cap of business achievements. I was now the owner of a company that was over a hundred years old, and one that I had greatly admired for more than thirty years. I was the one whom fate had chosen to bring this iconic brand back to glory and lead this historic company into the future.

Immediately upon purchase, I took all my knowledge and experience of working on and selling metalworking machinery and applied it to South Bend Lathe Company, coming out with high-end modern versions of lathes using the highest-grade components in the world. German and Japanese spindle bearings, American Allen-Bradley electronics and controls, Japanese inverters, the best internal gears... South Bend was a brand where additional money spent on high-end components would be easily recouped several times over at retail due to the confidence consumers had in it. We also kept a very large inventory of these high-quality machines on hand for same-day delivery. Industries that have a break-down or a need to replace an old machine right away cannot wait months for an order to come in.

Within a few short years, South Bend Lathe Company was once again thriving, once again a powerful and recognized name. Every single United States Navy ship launched today has at least one of our South Bend lathes on board, which helps crews make parts and maintain the ships while at sea. Numerous large industrial companies, the other branches of our military, schools, robotic labs, and other high-tech industries also own our new South Bend machines—even NASA has one. I have four South Bend lathes and milling machines in my personal shop at home—of course, all of them purchased at a deep discount!

The O'Brien brothers are probably smiling as they look down from heaven and see their company rise to greatness again.

South Bend Employees, 1920

South Bend Lathes in University of Notre Dame - 1930s

1926 South Bend Lathe

2020 South Bend Lathe

1920 South Bend Assembly Line

2020 South Bend Assembly Line

1920 O'Brien Brothers w/ South Bend Scaled Set

2020 Shiraz with Vintage South Bend Scaled Set

A Bad Case of Capitalism

CHAPTER 43

Butler Vs Balolia

In 2000, a guy named Steve Gass, a patent attorney and amateur woodworker with a doctorate in physics, designed and patented a device that electronically sensed human skin when it came in contact with the turning blade of a table saw. The device stopped the blade in milliseconds and dropped the blade below the tabletop. The only injury to the user would be a nick that could be covered with a band-aid.

The device was called a SawStop. Gass failed to license the technology to any manufacturer, so SawStop started having these saws made for them in a factory in Taiwan. Since Gass was a patent attorney, he registered more than a hundred patents on every possible function of the SawStop, making it impossible for anyone to copy his technology. Not everyone could afford a SawStop, as they were priced almost double that of regular table saws.

I contacted Gass numerous times over the years, asking if he would license his technology to me so we could produce Grizzly-branded table saws with the SawStop technology, to offer our customers a choice. We were unable to get any license from Gass for his invention. In addition, his company refused to sell us SawStop-branded table saws for us to sell to our customers.

Years passed, and I saw an article in a woodworking magazine about a device designed by a man named David Butler that could be a competing technology to SawStop. Butler claimed he had several patents for table-saw safety devices. For a long time, I'd been interested in making and selling products with improved safety. I contacted Butler for a possible purchase of his patent portfolio.

Most of my negotiations were with Butler's business advisor. After discussions, he and I agreed on a price for Butler's patent portfolio, subject to review by my patent attorney, since I was not equipped to evaluate the strength or scope of those patents. In the spring of 2012, Butler and I signed a letter of intent (LOI), which gave me time to review what I was proposing to purchase, and to decide whether to proceed to a purchase and sale agreement. To conduct that review, I hired a patent attorney I'd worked with before, who had a degree in electrical engineering. He reviewed Butler's patent portfolio, and also traveled to Massachusetts to meet with Butler and examine Butler's prototype inventions.

Based on his review, I concluded Butler's patent portfolio was not worth the price in the LOI (over $2 million). While I was willing to discuss purchasing the patent portfolio for a lower price, Butler's response was to file a lawsuit against me in Boston, claiming breach of contract, and asking to be paid the full amount in the LOI, even though there had been no purchase and nothing had been transferred to me.

The first federal judge assigned to the case dismissed it, holding that the LOI was not an enforceable contract. Butler appealed, and the appeals court reversed in part, allowing a portion of the lawsuit to continue.

The case was assigned to a new judge. My attorney was able to have more claims against me dismissed, leaving only a single claim to go to trial. The jury was asked to determine whether I had breached the LOI by failing to negotiate in good faith, and whether Butler and I would have entered into a purchase and sale agreement.

During the early years of the case, I had to travel to Boston for a day-long deposition, set for a total of eight hours as allowed by the judge. A deposition is where the opposing attorney is allowed to question me under oath in front of a court reporter who types every word into a stenograph machine. Often these reporters can type 300 words per minute. There is also a tape recorder as back-up. Anything said during a deposition can be uscd by either party during trial.

Butler's attorney was about 6'3" and physically fit. My own Boston lawyer, Laura Carroll, J.D. Cum Laude, Harvard Law School, had told me he played ice hockey in the evenings.

During the deposition, Butler's attorney could ask me anything he wanted: where I was born, how long I'd been in this country, if I were a U.S. citizen, what businesses I own, where I live. He was acting like a bully, and at one point my answer must have frustrated him because he said, "If you don't answer my question, I will keep you here for three days if I have to, to get my answer."

Keep in mind that everything was being recorded, and if I gave a combative answer, he would use that against me during trial. Despite his aggressive approach, I needed to reply with tact, at least while I was under oath.

I asked for a bathroom break. Since this was an official recess, the court reporter turned off her machine and stopped typing. At this point everything went off-record.

I pushed my chair back, leaned across the conference table toward Butler's attorney and said, "My flight leaves tomorrow morning and I plan on being on board. This deposition is set for eight hours, so you screaming that you'll keep me here for three days does not work for me."

Furious, he said I wasn't answering his questions.

My attorney Laura, who was enjoying the dialogue, jumped in, saying "My client is right. You can't keep him here past eight hours." She then proceeded to quote the exact law pertaining to this.

He turned red with anger as I walked out for my bathroom break.

The case went on for five years, with Butler's attorney filing various briefs and painting an evil picture of me. That was his job. The briefs before the judge went back and forth, with many appearances by our attorney. Butler's side won some rounds, and our side won some rounds, but nothing mattered up until the case went to trial before a judge and jury. That day came in the Fall of 2017. Leili and I flew to Boston for the culmination of the case. I'd been to Boston once before for the deposition day, and many years prior when my son Shabir graduated from Boston College. That was certainly a happier time.

I met with Laura for a couple of days' preparation before the trial. Laura was soft-spoken, motherly, and super-smart. Laura and Leili shared the same birthday, year and date. They hit it off immediately.

The courtroom was large and imposing, with oak benches behind two tables for the two parties facing the judge. Entering the courtroom through the oversized oak doors, you saw the jury box on the far right. The judge sat higher up in the middle with her back to the wall, facing the courtroom, at a grand desk on a raised platform. To the judge's right, lower, sat three law clerks. Next to them was the witness box, the same height as the judge's platform. A witness on this stand would face the jurors, and they would look straight at the witness. The witness stand had a microphone, and a screen for viewing exhibits during the trial.

The trial lasted for eight long days. Butler's attorney tried to make me out as this big, powerful businessman with lots of resources versus Butler, a military vet who was now 80 years old. The attorney portrayed his client as frail, but a couple of times after the case had ended for the day, Butler could be heard yelling at him.

One day during the trial when I was on the stand, I guessed exactly what Butler's attorney would ask, and how he would try to trap me. I had studied my deposition the night before in the hotel room and had a pretty good idea where he would go with his questioning. During a certain exchange, I answered what would have been his next question, only he hadn't asked it yet, and he probably didn't like the answer.

I must have come across as a little argumentative. He complained to the judge, who told me to stick to the exact question, and warned me to tone it down. I apologized to the judge. The attorney asked the next question, I gave the same answer that I had answered out of turn, and this time quoted the page and line number from my deposition even though I did not have a copy in front of me. It appeared that some of the jurors giggled. Butler's attorney must have been thinking out loud when he said, "It looks as if you know your deposition really well." Although I didn't say it, I thought *Mirror, mirror on the wall, who's the worst bully of them all*. Hahaha.

My attorney Laura's attitude was the polar opposite of the other attorney's aggression. She asked Butler softball questions on the stand and pretty soon it appeared as if he felt in charge. Then Laura would ask him to explain something he had done, and we would watch him squirm.

Laura had found some evidence where Butler had communication with the attorney for the USPTO. I don't remember exactly why, but Butler checked out this USPTO attorney's background, including where this government attorney lived, and put it all in an email to his business partner!

At trial, my attorney Laura was able to show that Butler had misrepresented his patent portfolio. Butler had been issued one patent, not several patents as he had claimed. In addition, one patent he had told me that was about to be issued by the USPTO had in fact been finally rejected by that office, before Butler had presented it to me as part of his claimed patent portfolio.

I won the lawsuit with a unanimous decision by the jury.

CHAPTER 44

Hobbies Galore!

I have always been good at working with my hands. As a boy in Mombasa, my mother taught me to sew. Mending was a useful skill, and one I would transfer, years later, to metalworking when I began to "mend" beat-up old machinery.

As a young teen in Mombasa, I took guitar lessons and learned how to play. I had no idea of it at the time, but with every moment of guitar practice, I was further developing that skill of working with my hands. At age 15, I even built a guitar for myself, using a hacksaw, file, sandpaper, and hand-operated drill (all hand tools).

As an older teen in Nairobi, I played bass in the school band and continued to play a lot of sports. I excelled at badminton, a sport requiring good hand-eye coordination, and became the school badminton captain. When Leili and I met at age 16, I was delighted to discover she was an excellent badminton player. In adulthood, we played as a mixed doubles team for many years, winning several tournaments. She is ambidextrous and was a killer at the net, while I covered the back.

My passion and skill for working with my hands led me into the business of selling machinery. I was interested in metalworking and woodworking, and over time I became very good at both.

As the years went by and I honed my skills, I was able to apply metalworking precision to building guitars. This was an area where the only limit was my imagination! To teach myself, I read several books on building guitars, and--since most of the large guitar-building companies in North America were customers of Grizzly--I was able to tour their facilities to see how they did it. I was fascinated to see how companies such as Taylor, Larrivee, Fender, and Gibson performed specific processes.

Today I can objectively say I can build guitars better than I can play them!

I approached each hobby with a level of intensity that would challenge me. Metalworking, woodworking, guitar-building, shooting—my passion for using my hands to create and excel fueled each hobby. I do not hunt, but shoot at paper when I shoot rifle, and at steel when I shoot pistol. My days of playing tournament-level badminton have come to an end, but my love of using machinery, as well as shooting, remains very strong.

Though I have a large workshop at home, I created another personal "dream shop" at Grizzly. Part of the reason Grizzly has been so successful is because I remain an advanced user of the machines we sell; that makes it very easy to view our products from the customer's perspective, as well as develop new products that our customers (like myself) would love.

My shop at Grizzly is a place where I can truly work and play at the same time.

Mother holding guitar I built with hand tools at age 15

Shiraz & Leili with badminton trophies at an awards ceremony

Quilted Maple "Tut" Acoustic Guitar Built by Shiraz
Numerous Inlays adorn this guitar. Mother of Pearl, Abalone, 18K Gold Necklace,
Ivory, and a One Carat Diamond in the Headdress

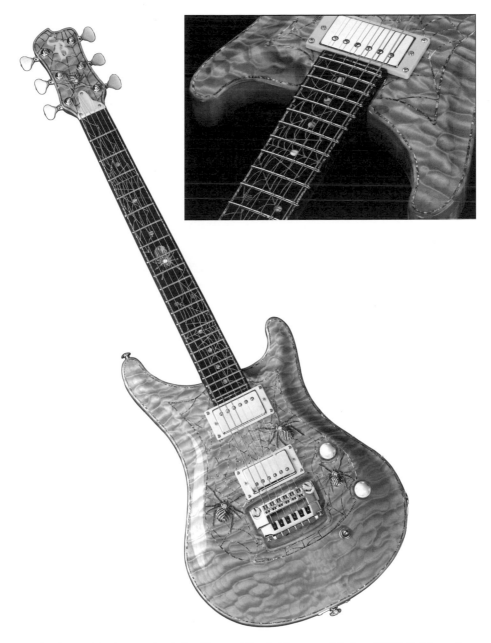

"Web of Jewels" Guitar Built by Shiraz. The Spiders are Made of 18K Gold, and Include Over 20 Carats of Emeralds, Sapphires, Rubies, and Diamonds.

"Flying Jewels" Guitar, Made by Shiraz. Butterflies are Loaded with Real Precious Stones and Set in 18K Gold.

"Two-Tone" Guitar, Built by Shiraz. Curly Maple & Curly Koa.

Box Shiraz Made for Leili for 20th Wedding Anniversary

Large "Forever" Boxes Made by Shiraz for Grandkids. Each Box is About 11" x 21".
Made of Bubinga and Guitar-Quality Maple. Completed 2020

Heavy-Duty 4 feet Long Bench Made by Shiraz for his Daughter out of Bubinga, with inlays of Ebony, Abalone and Mother of Pearl.

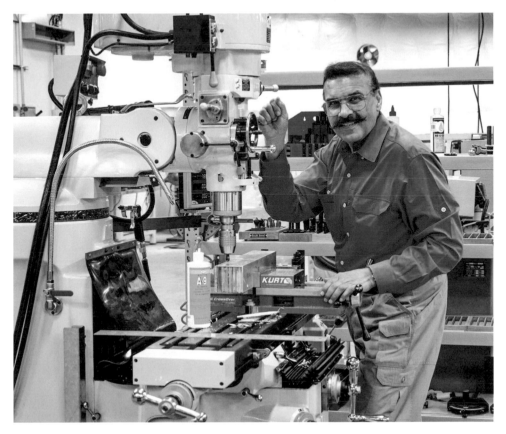

Shiraz Working on Mill

Shiraz in His Shop in Bellingham

A Bad Case of Capitalism

<u>CHAPTER 45</u>

Education and Employees

My father was a big believer in education. He sent all three of my older siblings to England to study, something made even more expensive because he had to convert his hard-earned money as an accountant from Kenyan shillings to British pounds. When it came my turn to be sent to England to study to become a chartered accountant (the British version of a CPA), I turned him down as I had something bigger to achieve: Leili. I wanted to get married, and against his objections, I refused to go to England to study further.

I have done well without a university education, and without any family or anyone else's help, but I have also had lady luck (my wife) by my side to support me in whatever I wanted to do. She never stopped me from starting new ventures, nor did she complain when some did not work out. She only said she never wanted me to be captain of the U.S. shooting team again. She felt I was traveling too much, running tryouts and doing other team tasks that took time away from her and from my businesses.

From my personal view, education is a necessity, and that is why I sent both of my kids through university. The problem arises when certain graduates think that since they now have a degree, life will be easy. Welcome to the real world! You have heard the saying "the harder I work, the luckier I get."

Over the years I have interviewed at least a thousand people for various positions in my business. In the beginning I occasionally hired college graduates straight out of college, but I soon found that these new graduates found their first real job to be too stressful, and they lasted a very short time with us. Many of them had apparently been primed by their professors, most of whom had never held a job outside of college, as to how the students' college degrees in a certain field made them eligible for management positions. Thus, many of the newly hired graduates thought that they should be promoted to management within the first six months of their tenure.

That's not how real business works. One must prove themselves in the environment that they're in, have patience, work hard, and good things will come. It seems there are many graduates coming out of colleges who feel they are owed something. This is not their fault, but that of some professors who theorize a perfect world in which a degree will open all doors. Even if those doors open, a degree or an MBA behind a name does not guarantee that person will work hard or make any meaningful contributions to the business.

More recently, some young people who are fresh out of college have the "sharing" mentality. They think that just because they work in a business (for which they are compensated) they should automatically share in the profits. This socialist-type thinking is shallow. The entrepreneur takes the risk by opening the business. The majority of such new businesses fail in the first year, sometimes taking the entrepreneur's life savings with it. Many businesses don't make much money for several years. Many lose money; you have seen my example of having lost millions in a business and then shutting it down. The entrepreneur makes the sacrifices and takes the risks. If the venture thrives, he or she reaps the rewards of success. If it fails, he or she could wind up bankrupt.

Other factors create unimaginable stress on a daily basis. Expensive lawsuits, employee problems, product shortages, recessions, product liability issues, recalls, government audits, etc. are all part of the headaches and challenges of a businessperson, plus you have no idea how much money an entrepreneur has lost in past businesses before having a successful one. When I started Grizzly, I put everything I had on the line. If Grizzly had failed, I would have been left penniless. If I had thought negatively about total failure before I started, I would never have begun. These are the risks and rewards of an entrepreneur, and the joys of living in a capitalistic society.

In my business, everything is merit-based. Work hard, bring new ideas, contribute to the growth of the company, put in your time, and you get rewarded with promotions and good pay. For many people, their work at Grizzly has become a rewarding, life-long career. My business model has been to lead by example; I would not ask anyone in my organization to do anything that I personally would not do. We come to work to get the job done, regardless of what the task entails. My Nanima (18 children champion grandmother) used to say, "There is no shame in work. If you are sweeping the floor, do it with pride and do a good job." We do not go to work to play with cell phones and be on social media for personal enjoyment. Someone is paying you for the time you spend at work, and it's called "work" for a reason.

However, once we are off duty, then it can be all play. Personally, when I am at home, I relax and enjoy my family's company, in a way I would not do at the office. At the company Christmas party, I tell jokes and show a different side of myself, because that's play time. When my daughter Jamila graduated from college and came to work for me, on her first day at work she came into my office in the afternoon and said, "Why are you so serious?" Up until then, she had only seen me in the role of a dad at home, joking and messing around. I said, "Jam—we are at work and we have a job to do. We can play around all we want at home, but over here we have to run a business and pay attention to everything."

Over the years I have tried to hire the brightest people I could. During interviews I concentrated on their tenure at companies as well as the positions they held in past jobs. Of course, I also paid attention to what kind of education they had, but education by itself was only a small fraction of my decision-making process.

One time I received a resume from a guy who had glowing letters of recommendation from almost every one of his past employers. His resume noted that he was a member of Mensa International, a society of people with extremely high IQ. The only problem was that all his past jobs had been shorter than six months. In those six months he had made himself so useful, and done so much for each business, that all were sorry to see him go and would take him back in a heartbeat. I wanted to meet this guy.

He came into my office well prepared for his interview (or maybe he did not prepare at all). He was a very presentable young man, about thirty years old, nicely dressed in a suit. As we talked, he asked a lot of good questions. He was grasping everything I was telling him about our processes and our expectations, and his answers were evolving positively through the interview. After about twenty minutes, he seemed to sense I was impressed with him and told me I would not be sorry if I hired him.

I said, "You are a dream employee for any company, but I am not going to hire you."

He raised his eyebrows as his face grew serious. "May I ask why?"

I said, "I know exactly what you're doing. You are going from business to business and learning everything about those businesses and their various processes, things you were not taught in college, and when you're satisfied with what you have learned, you will open your own business."

He broke into a big smile and said, "You're the first person that has figured me out."

I told him it was a pleasure meeting him and that he would indeed be very successful at whatever he did. He thanked me for my time.

We have many employees with very good educational backgrounds, but to advance within Grizzly and Woodstock they had to prove they could work hard in a regimented environment and get along with each other. We have over twenty managers, directors, and vice presidents in the company—every single one of these people, except for our CFO and director of marketing, was promoted from within. Several employees that were hired as warehouse employees moved up through the ranks and are now directors and managers within our company. In fact, Robert McCoy, an 18-year-old warehouse man I hired in 1989 at $5.50 an hour is now the president of Grizzly. He does not have a college degree, but he has good management skills, excellent logic, is respected by his co-workers, and has worked his butt off over the last thirty years.

On the other hand, I recently had a CFO who had several impressive degrees, but thought he was God's gift to mankind. He acted as if everybody in the place was a bumbling idiot. He got the boot in just a few short months.

The moral here is that no matter what your background or education is, if you work hard and apply yourself, you can be successful at whatever you do.

A Bad Case of Capitalism

CHAPTER 46

Knowledge is King

Throughout my journey, I have learned things that made me better as a person, better as a businessman, and better as a family man.

Of course, I've had regrets along the way, one of which is not having spent more time with my son Shabir as he was growing up. I missed many of his parent-teacher conferences that Leili attended, and some of his Tae Kwon Do tournaments (he is a black belt). I tried to rectify that when my daughter Jamila came along many years later, but it wasn't enough. All my life I've tried to balance my aggressiveness in business with family and personal hobbies, but sometimes one does not get the formula perfect.

As for succeeding in business, after the first couple of decades, it was no longer about making money. It was about growing market share and creating something out of nothing.

After purchasing the South Bend Lathe Company in 2009, I undertook several more business ventures. I started and closed Olivia and Henry Children's Boutique, an e-commerce business; started and closed March Optics, a high-end rifle scope company that made money but became a distraction where the effort did not justify the return; and started and closed Bullets.com, which sold brand-name shooting accessories and regularly lost a lot of money. (See comment about commodities, below.) I also started a couple of real estate ventures that are still active today and doing well.

I have no regrets about the businesses I opened and closed over the course of my career. (Over the decades, I launched twenty-nine businesses, eventually closing thirteen of them. I currently own sixteen operating businesses, of which the two largest by far are Grizzly Industrial and Woodstock International.) I accepted each failure as a learning experience, as a real-world lesson you cannot get any way other than by trying.

Some of the things I have learned:

If you're going to sell a product, do not sell just a commodity. If you sell someone else's brand-name product, numerous other sellers in the marketplace will be selling the identical item via various channels. Today, with Google and other price-checking sites instantly available on phones, these products become commodities, with the lowest price and fastest shipping winning the customer's business. This doesn't mean you should not sell these products at all, just that you should have proprietary items as well, to bring you more profit. Then you can sprinkle some commodity items in your offering.

Different people have different abilities and mindsets. You'll encounter people who are hardworking, or lazy, or diligent overachievers, or just average. In business, you try to draw out the best in your staff, find out what they're good at, and channel them into that area of your business. I always tried to run a well-regimented but fair business. Not everyone is cut out for such an environment, but those who are really thrive in it. My management team has an average tenure of more than nineteen years each within the company. They worked hard, proved to be an asset to the company and to their co-workers, and got promoted as the business grew. They recognized the benefits and stability of their jobs. Some of these managers' kids now work for us.

Negotiate hard. There is always a price "off the price list" when buying from a vendor. Be prepared to place larger orders to draw out the lower price. You can also negotiate early pay discounts of up to 2 percent. You make your money when you buy your products. When you sell it, this additional discount flows directly to your bottom line, so to speak.

Be honest and ethical in all dealings. If a vendor sends more product than you ordered, either keep it and pay for the additional product, or return it. Likewise, if they shipped less than what's shown on your invoice, by all means, take your deduction.

Pay your bills on time. I cannot stress this enough. As the saying goes, "beg, borrow, or steal," but pay your bills. (Obviously, don't take "steal" literally.) Paying bills like clockwork builds your reputation with vendors. It's easier to get new vendors to sell to you when you have a history of paying others on time.

Don't procrastinate. Get it off your plate so that you can concentrate on the next thing that comes at you. In business, as in life, things will constantly be spun at you, sometimes when you are least expecting them. Being caught up helps you deal with issues easier.

Don't be an absentee owner. You cannot expect others to run your business for you. I have seen so many failing businesses, from a simple juice bar to a corner grocery store to large companies where the owner is never around, and all kinds of issues occur in his or her absence.

Don't be intimidated by your employees' smarts. Embrace it, because when you surround yourself with smart people, they make jobs easier to tackle and make your organization successful.

Delegate work as you cannot do everything by yourself as your business grows. Don't assume what you have delegated is getting done. Keep your fingers in the system so you can catch issues that are going sideways quickly, not after the fact. In order to delegate, you must also first master the job.

Don't hold a grudge. All people make mistakes. When someone does, point it out but then let it go. Don't hold it against them in their job unless they are a repeat offender. If they're continually making mistakes, try to identify whether a certain situation is causing that, and see if there's another position within the company that's better suited for them. If not, then you have to part ways. Just because an employee does not work out with a company does not make you a bad company, or them a bad person. It just was not a good fit.

When you help the needy or do any charitable things, don't advertise it to make yourself look better. Do it to share what you have been blessed with, and to feel the satisfaction that brings.

Don't try to be everything to everyone. Sell a good selection of products but remain true to the core product line. When I started selling machines at Grizzly in 1983, my main core business was woodworking and metalworking machinery. That's mostly what we offered. I had a handful of necessary accessories, but thousands more accessories were added over the years as our finances got stronger, our staff levels increased, and our processes and organization improved. Starting with a large selection would have caused chaos and may have cost us success, as it did with Gorilla and Sons. On the other hand, don't be a "one item" company, as that will certainly spell disaster. Any kind of an issue will jeopardize the whole business.

Mentally compartmentalize your problems, as well as your stress, so it doesn't affect the rest of your progress. Problems in life, work, or business will always exist, just put them in a mental lockbox and deal with them one at a time.

Don't ever utter the words "this is not in my job description." Have a good attitude about work or whatever task you have been given and give it your best without complaining. Complainers and whiners don't get far in life. In all the years, never once have I promoted a person with a bad attitude. We try to counsel them, but when we are unsuccessful at turning around attitudes, they do not last in our organization. A bad apple can affect others around them and cause more issues down the road.

Don't be afraid of getting your hands dirty. Lead by example. Menial tasks exist in every walk of life and they need to be done. If you expect your employees to respect you as a boss and a person, you need to earn that respect. I feel that my people respect me because I have done, and will do, anything that I ask them to do. From running the forklifts, to picking and packing orders, to getting on my knees and showing the service tech how to weld, to cleaning bathrooms – I have done it all, without any qualms.

As the boss, be prepared to make hard decisions. Do not get emotionally attached to an idea, process, product or supplier. If things aren't going well, evaluate the situation with an open mind and make a logical, fact-based decision. You may have to cut your losses and re-direct your time and energy towards something that brings in better returns.

Don't look down on co-workers or employees. You may be very smart, have some great education, but nothing beats real-world experience, logic, and a good attitude. Consider every failure a learning experience. When you get knocked down, get up, and try again.

Over the decades in business and other ventures, I have learned many things the hard way and hope that you found some of the above tips helpful.

Writing this autobiography made me re-live many things I had shut out of my mind. At times, there was sadness as I recalled some things from the early days. However, as I retraced my steps through the years, I have remembered many happy and wonderful moments.

I've lived my life with a wide-open throttle, with pedal to the metal, and it feels as if I have lived through several lifetimes in one. As far as my machinery business goes, it is a hobby gone wild!

Thank you for reading about my life.

Timeline

1952 to 1968	Childhood in Mombasa, Kenya.
1969	I move to Nairobi for A-levels, the last two years in the British school system.
1970	Father sends older brother Anil to settle in Vancouver, Canada. Other family to follow.
1972	I join Anil in Vancouver; Leili moves to Vancouver; we marry; I manage Busy Bee Dry Cleaners.
1975	I meet Wolf Heidemann at shooting range; I discover lathes.
1975	I borrow $500 to start buying and selling used lathes.
1976	I incorporate Busy Bee Machine Tools. I expand to new machines.
1977	I contact a manufacturer in Taiwan; I attend first trade show there.
1978	Father insists I take on brother as partner; I refuse and close Busy Bee Machine Tools; I move to San Diego to start new business.
1979	I am invited to join family's new business. I return to Vancouver.
1980	I publish the first machinery catalog in Canada.
1981	I send sample planer to Taiwan.
1983	I sell my interest in family business in Vancouver.

1983	I incorporate Grizzly Imports in Bellingham, Washington; I rent a warehouse on Meridian Street.
1986	Grizzly buys the Shell Building in Williamsport, Pennsylvania; we open in January 1987.
1986	Our immigration into U.S. finalizes; I move with wife and children from Vancouver to Bellingham.
1987	I incorporate mail-order jewelry business Elite Exclusives; I close it two years later.
1989	Grizzly moves into new headquarters on Valencia Street in Bellingham. I incorporate Woodstock International. I hire Robert McCoy, an 18-year-old warehouse man. I acquire Cascade Tools.
1990	With Chris and Gail Bach, I form Balolia Bach Properties to buy Allan Island.
1991	I incorporate Elite Developments, a real estate company in Bellingham.
1992	Balolia Bach Properties closes sale of Allan Island to Paul Allen of Microsoft.
1993	I acquire Dollar Trading Company; Magna-set; and Pro-Stik. I incorporate Sculptures of Venice.
1994	I incorporate Grizzly Knife & Tackle. I acquire Gutmann Cutlery. I incorporate Gorilla and Sons.
1995	Woodstock makes Inc. magazine's top 500 companies due to rate of growth in the U.S.
1996	Woodstock makes Inc. magazine's top 500 again.
1996	Grizzly becomes first machinery company with an internet website, grizzlyimports.com.

1997	Grizzly opens Memphis facility; we close it 18 months later. I close Gorilla and Sons.
1998	Grizzly Imports becomes Grizzly Industrial. Grizzly opens quality-control office in Taiwan.
1999	Grizzly builds a facility in Springfield, Missouri.
2000	I acquire domain name Grizzly.com. Grizzly acquires additional land in Springfield, builds a second facility there. Grizzly opens office in Shanghai.
2001	Grizzly builds a facility in Muncy, Pennsylvania; sells Shell Building in Williamsport.
2006	Grizzly builds a second facility in Bellingham.
2008	Grizzly builds a second facility in Muncy.
2009	I acquire South Bend Lathe Company.
2015	We close the Muncy facility and consolidate main distribution through Springfield.
2015 to 2019	I incorporate six more businesses, of which three remain.
2020	I transition to Chairman and CEO. Robert McCoy becomes President. In total, Grizzly and Woodstock operate out of 860,000 sq ft of warehouse space on 68 acres in two locations, with 300 employees in U.S. and over a dozen in China and Taiwan.

Lifelong Gratitude

They say that behind every successful man is a woman. As a kid I used to be dismissive when I heard that old saying, but as I write this book and recount everything that went on in my life, I can say with absolute certainty that I could not have done it without the support of my wife, Leili.

She has been the pillar that kept me sane all these years when there were major issues in business. Often, I would bounce off ideas and discuss problems with her and many times she would come up with a solution that I had not thought of.

Besides that, she stayed at home and took care of our children from the moment they were born, never relying on a single babysitter to do that job. She is a caring mother, an incredible cook, and my personal "doctor," giving me natural medicines and herbs that have kept me heathy all these years. She even gave me countless massages when I returned home late at night after working long hours. She took care of the home front so I would not have to worry about anything.

Leili has been the greatest life partner one could ever hope for. I got really lucky!

Thank you, Leili!

Acknowledgement

I would like to thank Cheryl Stritzel McCarthy for helping me with this book. I met her when she wrote an article on me for a local magazine.

Cheryl edited my work, prodded me for details that I would never have thought of and guided me on chapter layout and other details throughout the writing process. She mentioned things about writing a book that I would otherwise not have known. For example, I would talk about a courtroom and go straight into describing what happened, but she would ask me about the kind of furniture and what I saw as I entered the courtroom, to bring the reader into the courtroom with me. If I was taking a drive in Congo, what did I see? If I talked about breakfast, what did I eat? It was all these details that she forced me to remember. Heck, she even strongly, but politely, suggested I sanitize my graphic description of what happened in Memphis. What you read was the sanitized, toned-down version.

Thank you, Cheryl.

About the Author

Shiraz Balolia started his first company after he saw a friend's lathe, a metalworking machine, and wanted one for himself but did not have the money. He borrowed $500 to buy used lathes to fix and sell, figuring if he did that enough times, he'd eventually clear enough profit to buy a lathe for himself.

That beginning, at age twenty-three in 1975 in Vancouver, Canada, led to other endeavors that would eventually become a very large business.

Shiraz was born in 1952 in Kenya to parents of Indian heritage, and left Kenya in 1972 for Canada, where his sweetheart, Leili, soon joined him and they married.

Shiraz founded Grizzly Imports in Bellingham, Washington, in 1983, moving there with Leili and their two children, eventually gaining United States citizenship. Now called Grizzly Industrial, the machinery and tools company's customers include Boeing, Ford Motor Company, NASA, and the U.S. military. In 1989, Shiraz launched Woodstock International to sell to other dealers, and continued to expand, opening facilities in Pennsylvania and Missouri. Grizzly and Woodstock now have over 860,000 square feet of warehouse space on sixty-eight acres of its own land.

Starting with nothing, Shiraz eventually launched twenty-nine businesses. Today he owns sixteen companies, including Grizzly Industrial, which has annual revenue in nine figures, 300 employees, and offices in Taiwan and Shanghai. His twenty-plus managers have an average tenure of nineteen years with his companies. He currently holds four patents.

Shiraz remains an advanced user of woodworking and metalworking machines, building everything from guitars to keepsake boxes for his four grandchildren.

He is an accomplished long-distance marksman, having shot in three world championships and won numerous gold medals at 1000-yards distance.

Shiraz's Shooting Biography

Shiraz has been shooting pistols, rifles and shotguns for over 40 years and has been involved in long range rifle shooting at the National and International level for over 10 years. He served as the Captain of the United States F-Class Open Rifle Team for the 2013 World Championship, and is a four time US National Champion in a four man team at 1000 yards, and a three time Canadian National Champion at 700, 800 and 900 Meters. He has won numerous gold medals in long range shooting, has set several National records, and was recently awarded Distinguished Rifleman, the highest honor in shooting!

Three time Washington State F-Class Champion

2007   Appointed to Vice-Captain of the United States F-Class Open Rifle Team

2008   Gold medal USA / European Team match

2009   Represented U.S.A. at the F-Class World Championships in Bisley, England. Came home with bronze, silver and gold medals in various categories

2009   Gold medal, Team USA, four man International Team match, Bisley, England

2010   Gold medal at 1000 yards, United States F-Class National Championships

2011   Appointed as Captain of United States F-Class Open Rifle Team

2012   Gold medal at 1000 yards, United States F-Class National Championships

2013   Match winner and gold medal, F-Open, Berger Southwest Long Range Rifle Championships at Phoenix, Arizona, 800, 900, 1000 yards

2013 Match winner F-Open, Rocky Mountain Palma Championships at Raton, New Mexico, 800, 900, 1000 yards

2013 Gold medal, four man team match United States National Championship, 1000 yards

2014 Gold medal, four man team match, Berger SW Nationals

2014 Team Grizzly sets a national record at 800, 900, 1000 yards.

2014 Gold Medal and National Champion of Canadian F-Class National Championships, Ottawa 700, 800 & 900 Meters.

2014 Gold Medals in all 3 Four-Man Team matches at Canadian F-Class National Championships in Ottawa

2014 Represented USA National Team and won gold medal at the America Match against the Canadians

2014 Gold Medal 1000 Yards at 2014 United States F-Class Nationals

2014 Gold Medal 1000 Yards Four-Man Team match (Team Grizzly), United States F-Class Championship

2015 Gold Medal and National Champion 700, 800, 900 Meters at Canadian National Championships in Ottawa

2015 Gold Medal 1000 Yards at 2015 United States National Championships.

2015 Gold Medal 1000 Yards Four-Man Team Match (Team Grizzly) United States F-Class Championship.

2016 Remarkable third consecutive Canadian F-Class National Championship win 2016, 2015, 2014 in Ottawa.

2017 Gold Medal, 4-Man Team Match (Team USA), Canadian National Championship. 700, 800, 900 Meters. Teams from 13 Countries Competed in this Huge Match.

2018 Won a gold medal at the United States F-Class Championships at 1000 yards, shooting an incredible 200-14x. (14 of his 20 shots were inside a 5" x ring at 1000 yards)

2018 Gold Medal, 1000 Yards Four Man Team Match, United States F-Class Open Team Championship.

2018 Awarded International Distinguished Rifleman Award, the highest
and most prestigious award given to a rifleman in the USA.
Certified as a high master by the NRA in Long Range, Mid-Range
and Full Bore F-Class shooting, the highest classification in
rifle shooting. Holder of several national records in
F-Class competition